Paragraphs
for
Elementary School

Paragraphs
for
Elementary School

A Sentence-Composing Approach

A Student Worktext

Don and Jenny Killgallon

HEINEMANN
Portsmouth, NH

Heinemann

145 Maplewood Ave., Suite 300

Portsmouth, NH 03801

www.heinemann.com

Offices and agents throughout the world

Library of Congress Cataloging-in-Publication Data
Killgallon, Don.
  Paragraphs for elementary school / Don and Jenny Killgallon.
     pages cm
   ISBN 978-0-325-04794-2
1. English language—Paragraphs—Problems, exercises, etc. 2. English language—Sentences—Problems, exercises, etc. 3. English language—Rhetoric—Problems, exercises, etc. 4. Report writing—Problems, exercises, etc. I. Killgallon, Jenny. II. Title.

PE1439.K54 2014
372.62'3044—dc23   2013049042

Editor: Tobey Antao
Production: Sonja S. Chapman
Interior and cover designs: Monica Ann Crigler
Typesetter: Cape Cod Compositors, Inc.
Manufacturing: Steve Bernier

Printed in the United States of America on acid-free paper
          3   4   5   GP   21   22   23   24

To elementary school teachers for laying the foundation for lifelong learning through teaching reading and writing.

CONTENTS

EXERCISING PARAGRAPH MUSCLES

This book is a training program for better writing. Your instructors are famous authors. On each page, they train you to build stronger sentences and paragraphs.

A paragraph contains linked sentences about the same topic and is built like a tree with branches attached to the trunk. The trunk is the topic of the paragraph, and the branches are the sentences attached to that topic.

Good paragraphs contain linked sentences, like a bowl containing cornflakes, milk, sugar. Bad paragraphs don't contain linked sentences, like a bowl containing cornflakes, raw hamburger, vinegar.

EXERCISING SENTENCE MUSCLES

There are just two parts needed for a sentence: a subject (the topic of the sentence) and a predicate (a comment about the subject).

Writing is carpentry with sentences and paragraphs. Like any craft, it is only as good as the plans, materials, and tools you use. Here you will learn, practice, and use tools to build better sentences for your paragraphs.

CHUNKING SENTENCES 61

Sentences have chunks of meaning. Chunks are sentence parts that add detail and information and style. Good sentences like those by authors are really chunky.

IMITATING SENTENCES 70

Authors, your fitness trainers in writing, show you the shape of sentences, and you imitate the same shape in your sentences. Those author-trainers show you how, and then you do it.

UNSCRAMBLING SENTENCES 83

This activity is like solving a jigsaw puzzle by arranging the pieces of the puzzle to create a good picture. Here, though, you arrange scrambled sentence parts to build a good sentence.

BUILDING STRONG PARAGRAPHS

VARYING PARAGRAPHS 91

Variety is the spice of life. In this section, you'll practice ways to add spice within your paragraphs through variety in sentence-composing tools.

IMITATING PARAGRAPHS 99

Now you move on from sentences to paragraphs. You learn how to build stronger paragraphs by imitating ones by your author-trainers in your writing fitness program.

UNSCRAMBLING PARAGRAPHS 120

Good paragraphs arrange sentences in ways that make sense to your readers. Unscrambling paragraphs is good practice for building stronger paragraphs.

PUTTING PARAGRAPHS TO WORK 134

People have different jobs because there's lots of things that need doing. Paragraphs also have different jobs because there's lots of things that need understanding.

ADDING PIZZAZZ 141

Anything with pizzazz is always attractive, often dazzling, certainly memorable. Adding details to sentences and paragraphs creates pizzazz.

PARTYING WITH SENTENCES AND PARAGRAPHS 161

THANKING YOUR WRITING FITNESS TRAINERS 162

These authors—over three hundred of them—provided your training in this writing fitness program by modeling how to write sentences and paragraphs like theirs.

WITH GRATITUDE

Thanks, deep and wide, to the hundreds of authors within—your trainers in this writing fitness program—for modeling good writing by showing you the way to build stronger sentences and paragraphs.

Their names are on pages 162–169. Mind your manners. Thank them—and of course also your teacher—for helping you become a better writer.

HELLO

PLAYING WITH SENTENCES AND PARAGRAPHS

*In writing sentences or paragraphs
there should always be an element of play.*

—Thornton Wilder, *writer*

Host of the children's TV show *Mr. Rogers' Neighborhood*, Fred Rogers said, "Play is often talked about as if it were a relief from serious learning, but for children play is serious learning. Play is really the work of childhood."

Authors play with sentences and paragraphs, trying different lengths, arrangements, and styles to seriously discover their best writing. Playing is actually creating because it results in something new, different, interesting.

Like those authors, within the exercises of this book, you'll play with sentences and paragraphs to seriously learn how to build better sentences and paragraphs.

PARAGRAPH TRAINING PROGRAM

Do you remember how you learned to talk? As a baby, you used your voice to make sounds, to coo, and sometimes to cry, but, at first, you couldn't use it to talk. You may have heard the saying, "You have to crawl before you can walk." Well, you have to coo before you can talk, too.

What helped you to go from crawling to walking, from cooing to talking? You had teachers who showed you how. They were probably your parents or others who loved you and wanted to help you. For walking, they modeled how to walk as you watched them, guided you, and held you up when you took your first steps, picked you up when you fell, and coached you and cheered you until you were walking on your own. Through imitating your parents, who modeled how to walk, you went from baby steps to walking.

How did you learn to go from cooing to talking? You had teachers there, too, who modeled how to talk. As you listened, they mentored you by pronouncing words and then listening to you say them and correcting you when you made mistakes. You went from gibberish to language.

Walking uses muscles. Learning to walk requires training those muscles to behave in ways that allow confident walking, without falling. Think of the exercises in this worktext as a training program to strengthen your writing muscles so that you can build better sentences and paragraphs. Like any successful athlete, you'll go through rigorous practice sessions. Those sessions will help you build your writing muscles and learn how to imitate your expert trainers in writing better sentences and paragraphs.

A trainer is someone who knows very well how to do something and can show you how to do it, too. In learning to write better, those trainers in the exercises in this book are authors. In your training program, you'll be trained by authors of successful books like *Charlotte's Web*, *The Secret Garden*, *Harry Potter*, *Charlie and the Chocolate Factory*, *The Hunger Games*, *Ender's Game*, *Matilda*, and hundreds more.

Set your goal to learn to build your sentences and paragraphs like those of your trainers. Like any training, sometimes it won't be easy, but it will always be helpful, and sometimes fun, too. The goal is worth it because learning to write better is important in and beyond school.

Good writers say more. In this worktext, you will train to learn the sentence-composing tools they use to say more. As a result, you will build strong sentences and paragraphs. *Paragraphs for Elementary School: A Sentence-Composing Approach* gives you a toolbox to take with you whenever you write.

Read these two paragraphs. The weak one doesn't use those tools. The strong one does.

WEAK PARAGRAPH

(1) He ran down the mountain path. (2) Several times he fell, but was on his feet again in the next breath. (3) He fell hard onto his face.

STRONG PARAGRAPH

(1) Blindly, he ran down the mountain path, heedless of the rocks and shrubs. (2) Several times he fell, but was on his feet again in the next breath, stumbling, tripping, skidding in a head-long descent. (3) When at last he reached the point where the path leveled out, he fell hard onto his face, the dirt mixing with his tears, his teeth cutting into his top lip, causing him to spit blood. (adapted)

Linda Sue Park, *A Single Shard*

The underlined parts add information. (The word for saying more is *elaboration*.) Elaboration builds more detailed sentences, like ones by authors. You can use the same tools as authors to say more in your sentences and paragraphs. Through their sentences and their paragraphs, those hundreds of authors are ready to train you with the equipment and tools you'll need to build stronger sentences and paragraphs.

Often, students don't say more because they don't have the tools for elaboration. A major goal of *Paragraphs for Elementary School: A Sentence-*

Composing Approach is to help you learn tools for elaboration within your sentences and paragraphs.

In the exercises in this book, you'll see how over three hundred authors shaped and built their sentences and paragraphs. You'll learn how you can shape and build your own sentences and paragraphs like theirs. Those authors are your invisible fitness trainers in building stronger writing muscles.

I threw words all over the place,
and none of them landed right.

—Pat Conroy, *My Reading Life*

Learn everything you can from your writing fitness trainers, as they train you to build better sentences and paragraphs using sentence-composing tools like the ones they use. If you do, your words, after you throw them, will land right.

In the writing Olympics, your trainers are gold-medal winners. As you begin your writing fitness program, train like an Olympic athlete. Sometimes it will be hard work, but getting a gold medal is worth it.

PARAGRAPH PRIMER

What does a paragraph look like? It's the block of text with the first line indented. That indentation says to readers, "Here's something new and different from the last paragraph." That's what a paragraph looks like.

What does a paragraph do? It contains sentences all linked to the same topic: an idea, a place, a person, a process, a story, an explanation, a description. That's what a paragraph does.

How is a paragraph built? It is built like a tree, with branches attached to the trunk. The trunk is the topic the paragraph is about, and the branches are the sentences linked to that topic. That's what a paragraph is built like.

Look at the above three paragraphs. The topic of the first is what a paragraph looks like, with a series of linked sentences telling you what it looks like. The topic of the second paragraph is what a paragraph does, with a series of linked sentences telling you what it does. The topic of the third paragraph is what a paragraph is built like, with a series of linked sentences telling you about that topic.

You DO not have a topic sentence for each paragraph

Sometimes the first sentence of a paragraph previews what the paragraph is about, the way a trailer previews what a movie is about. That sentence announces the topic of the paragraph, so it's called a "topic sentence." After the paragraph's topic sentence are sentences linked to that topic.

Here is an example with two paragraphs, a description of why Hazel misses her old school and dislikes her new school. The preview sentences tell the topic of each paragraph, and the linked sentences fill in the details.

Hazel's first year at Lovelace Elementary was very different from her old school. In her other school, the classrooms didn't have desks. They called their teachers by their first names. Hazel tried that with Mrs. Jacobs on her first day at Lovelace. It did not go over well. The good thing was she now went to the same school as Jack.

The bad thing was everything else. Hazel did not like sitting at a desk. She did not like having to call her teacher Mrs. Anything. She did not like homework and work sheets and fill-in-the-blank and multiple-choice. In her old school teachers said she was so creative and imaginative, and now all she heard was that she did not do assignments and needed to learn to follow school rules.

Anne Ursu, *Breadcrumbs*

The topic of the first paragraph is in its first sentence: differences between Hazel's old school and her new school. Notice how the sentences after the preview sentence link to that topic. The linked sentences tell what things Hazel liked about her old school, how those things were unwelcome in her new school, and how there was just one thing she liked about her new school.

The topic of the second paragraph is also previewed in its first sentence: things in the new school she doesn't like. Notice how the sentences after the preview sentence link to that topic. The linked sentences list all the "bad things" about the new school.

EXERCISE 1: SELECTING PARAGRAPH TITLES

As a way to tell whether you understand what the paragraph says, select the best title for the paragraph. The title you select should sum up most of what the paragraph says. Jot down reasons for your choice.

PARAGRAPH ONE

It snowed fluffy white flakes big enough to show their crystal architecture, like perfect geometric poems. It was the sort of snow that transforms the world around it into a different kind of place. You know what it's like when you wake up to find everything white and soft and quiet, when you run outside and your breath suddenly appears before you in a smoky poof, when you wonder for a moment if the world in which you woke up is not the same one that you went to bed in the night before. Things like that happen, at least in the stories you read. It was the sort of snowfall that, if there were any magic to be had in the world, would make it come out.

Anne Ursu, *Breadcrumbs*

What is the best title for this paragraph?
a. Winter Snow

b. Lovely White

c. White Magic

PARAGRAPH TWO

Papa handed Esperanza the knife. The short blade was curved like a scythe, its fat wooden handle fitting snugly in her palm. This job was usually reserved for the eldest son of a wealthy rancher, but since Esperanza was an only child and Papa's pride and glory, she was always given the honor. Last night she had watched Papa sharpen the knife back and forth across a stone, so she knew the tool was edged like a razor.

Pam Muñoz Ryan, *Esperanza Rising*

What is the best title for this paragraph?
a. Esperanza's Sharp Knife

b. A Knife to Honor Esperanza

c. Preparations of Esperanza's Knife

PARAGRAPH THREE

When I think back on it, I'd have to say that it all started with the Golden Lotus. The Golden Lotus is a famous Chinese restaurant, about two hours away from where I live. It is a long way to go for dinner, as Mom pointed out to Dad when his cousin first invited us to come for a birthday party.

Wendy Wan-Long Shang, *The Great Wall of Lucy Wu*

What is the best title for this paragraph?

a. A Wonderful Birthday Party

b. Fun at Golden Lotus

c. Looking Back

PARAGRAPH FOUR

The wheels of the skateboard made a rumbling hum as they rolled over the pavement at the little town park. I loved that sound. The world rushed by me as I zipped across the blacktop. I could feel how smooth or rough it was right through my sneakers, and it was like I was watching the park in fast-forward. The greens and browns of the grass and trees flashed by on the sides as I kept my eyes on the little concrete path in front of me, looking for the next good, flat spot. I was trying to get this one trick down, but the board wasn't cooperating. It slipped out from under me again and went bouncing across the ground.

Amar'e Stoudemire, *STAT: Home Court*

What is the best title for this paragraph?

a. Through My Sneakers

b. Skateboarding in the Park

c. Finding a Flat Spot

PARAGRAPH FIVE

He was overweight, and the kids at his middle school often teased him about his size. Even his teachers sometimes made cruel comments without realizing it. On his last day of school, his math teacher, Mrs. Bell, taught ratios. As an example she chose the heaviest kid in the class and the lightest kid in the class, and had them weigh themselves. Stanley weighed three times as much as the other boy. Mrs. Bell wrote the ratio on the board, 3:1, unaware of how much embarrassment she had caused both of them.

Louis Sachar, *Holes*

What is the best title for this paragraph?
a. Overweight Children

b. Last Day of School

c. A Bad Math Class

EXERCISE 2: CREATING PARAGRAPH TITLES

To test your understanding, give each paragraph a title that sums up what the paragraph is mainly about. For each paragraph, create a good title, and share it with classmates to see how they titled the same paragraph. Maybe the class could hold a contest to choose the best titles. *Be sure to correctly capitalize your titles.*

PARAGRAPH ONE

Luke went over to the kitchen window and peered out at the woods, trying for the umpteenth time to picture rows and rows of houses where the firs and maples and oaks now stood—or rather had stood. Luke knew that half the trees were now toppled. Some already lay on the ground. Some hung at weird angles from their former lofty positions in the sky. Their absence made everything look different, like a fresh haircut exposing a band of untanned skin on a forehead. Even from deep inside the kitchen, Luke could tell the trees were missing because everything was brighter, more open, but scarier.

Margaret Peterson Haddix, *Among the Hidden*

PARAGRAPH TWO

The bell rang. Everyone signed off their desks or hurriedly typed in reminders to themselves. Some were dumping lessons or data into their computers at home. A few gathered at the printers while something they wanted to show was printed out. Ender spread his hands over the child-size keyboard near the edge of the desk and wondered what it would feel like to have hands as large as a grown-up's. They must feel so big and awkward, thick stubby fingers and beefy palms. Of course, they had bigger keyboards—but how could their thick fingers draw a fine line, the way Ender could, a thin line so precise that he could make it spiral seventy-nine times from the center to the edge of the desk without the lines ever touching or overlapping. It gave him something to do while the teacher droned on about arithmetic.

Orson Scott Card, *Ender's Game*

PARAGRAPH THREE

It is a neat office. It has a desk tucked snug under the hot-water pipe and walls covered in pegboard. Uncle Potluck in his office hangs his tools on those walls. He's drawn white lines around them, too, like the ones they draw around dead bodies on TV shows, except dead-body lines are about mysteries, and Uncle Potluck's lines are about things being for sure where they belong, the broom in the broom spot, the wrench in the wrench spot. There's even a white outline for Uncle Potluck's hat, although that spot mostly stays empty. Things that don't belong on the walls have shelf spots or drawer spots, all of them neatly labeled.

Linda Urban, *Hound Dog True*

PARAGRAPH FOUR

It is the nightly custom of every good mother after her children are asleep to rummage in their minds and put things straight for next morning, repacking into their proper places the many articles that have wandered during the day. If you could keep awake, you would see your own mother doing this, and you would find it very interesting to watch her. It is quite like tidying up drawers. You would see her on her knees, lingering humorously over some of your contents, wondering where on earth you had picked this thing up, making discoveries sweet and not so sweet, pressing this to her cheek as if it were as nice as a kite, and hurriedly stowing that out of sight. When you wake in the morning, the naughtiness and evil passions with which you went to bed have been folded up small and placed at the bottom of your mind; and on the top, beautifully aired, are spread out your prettier thoughts, ready for you to put on.

J. M. Barrie, *Peter Pan*

PARAGRAPH FIVE

The rain poured down on London so hard that it seemed that it was dancing spray, every raindrop contending with its fellows for supremacy in the air and waiting to splash down. It was a deluge. The drains and sewers were overflowing, throwing up the debris of muck, slime, and filth, the dead dogs, the dead rats, cats, and worse, bringing back up to the world of men all those things that they thought they had left behind them, jostling and bubbling and churning like some nameless soup boiling in a dreadful cauldron.

Terry Pratchett, *Dodger*

EXERCISE 3: ARRANGING PARAGRAPHS

Underneath the paragraph are two sentences. What sentence should be the paragraph's first sentence? What sentence should be the paragraph's last sentence?

PARAGRAPH ONE (from "The Scarlet Ibis" by James Hurst)

Summary: The younger brother, nicknamed Doodle, almost died after being born.

(1) It was, though, a nice crazy, like someone you meet in your dreams. (2) He was born when I was six and was, from the outset, a disappointment. (3) He seemed all head, with a tiny body which was red and shriveled like an old man's. (4) Everybody thought he was going to die. (5) Daddy had Mr. Heath, the carpenter, build a little mahogany coffin for him. (6) But he didn't die, and when he was three months old, Mama and Daddy decided they might as well name him. (7) They named him William Armstrong, which was like tying a big tail on a small kite.

Choices

a. Such a name sounds good only on a tombstone.

b. Doodle was just about the craziest brother a boy ever had.

PARAGRAPH TWO (from *Barrio Boy* by Ernesto Galarza)

Summary: A Mexican, new in America, comments on a difference between Mexicans and Americans.

They did not listen if you did not speak loudly, as they always did. In the Mexican style, people would know that you were enjoying their jokes tremendously if you merely smiled and shook a little, as if you were trying to swallow your mirth. In the American style there was little difference between a laugh and a roar.

Choices

a. Until you got used to them, you could hardly tell whether the boisterous Americans were roaring mad or roaring happy.

b. We had to get used to the Americans.

PARAGRAPH THREE (from *War Horse* by Michael Morpurgo)

Summary: Told from the point of view of a horse, this is the first meeting between that horse and his young owner Albert.

(1) I jumped at first when he touched me but could see at once that he meant me no harm. (2) He smoothed my back first and then my neck, talking all the time about what a fine time we would have together, how I would grow up to be the smartest horse in the whole wide world, and how we would go out hunting together. (3) After a bit, he began to rub me gently with his coat. (4) He rubbed me until I was dry and then dabbed salt water onto my face where the skin had been rubbed raw. (5) He brought in some sweet hay and a bucket of cool water. (6) I do not believe he stopped talking the whole time.

Choices

a. Albert was about my height, and talked so gently as he approached me that I was immediately calmed and a little intrigued so stood where I was against the wall.

b. As he turned to go out of the stable, I called out to him to thank him, and he seemed to understand for he smiled broadly and stroked my nose.

PARAGRAPH FOUR
(from *The Talking Earth* by Jean Craighead George)

Summary: A huge alligator attempts to attack a boat containing a young girl.

(1) It was sheathed in heavy armor and spiked with sharp ridges. (2) The monstrous tail came straight toward her. (3) She dropped to the bottom of the dugout as a mammoth alligator struck the stern of the boat and catapulted it forward. (4) It rocked, tipped, but not quite over, then hit the beach with a crack. (5) She jumped ashore as a fifteen-foot alligator slammed his jaws closed on the rear of the boat.

Choices

a. The wood splintered.

b. Out of the water in the everglades rose a tail so large it could have belonged to a whale.

PARAGRAPH FIVE (from *The Hunger Games* by Suzanne Collins)

Summary: Older sister Katniss describes the cat belonging to Prim, her little sister.

(1) Prim named him Buttercup, insisting that his muddy yellow coat matched the bright flower. (2) He hates me. (3) I think he still remembers how I tried to drown him in a bucket when Prim brought him home, a scrawny kitten, belly swollen with worms, crawling with fleas. (4) The last thing I needed was another mouth to feed. (5) But Prim begged so hard, cried even, I had to let him stay. (6) It turned out okay. (7) My mother got rid of the vermin and he's a born mouser. (8) Even catches the occasional rat. (9) Sometimes, when I clean a kill, I feed Buttercup the entrails. (10) He has stopped hissing at me.

Choices

a. This is the closest we will ever come to love.

b. Sitting in bed at Prim's knees, guarding her, is the world's ugliest cat, with mashed-in nose, half of one ear missing, eyes the color of rotting squash.

REVIEW

A paragraph is a block of information with linked sentences telling about the same topic. It's like an Internet search for a topic, with all hits.

PREVIEW

The sentences in a paragraph tell more about the paragraph's topic in a meaningful arrangement of well-built sentences. It's like a cluster of grapes connected to the same stem.

PARAGRAPH LINKS

Containers hold things. Boxes, crates, baskets, drawers contain things: a box of candy, a crate with furniture, a basket of fruit, a drawer for socks, and so forth. A paragraph contains a series of *linked* sentences. A series is one thing occurring after another thing. In a paragraph, one sentence occurs after another. If sentences are linked, they all are connected to the topic of the paragraph. To be a paragraph, sentences must be linked in a clear arrangement and share the same purpose. If they are not linked nor clearly arranged, there is no paragraph—just a jumble of unlinked sentences making no sense and having no clear purpose.

Notice that the preceding paragraph has clearly linked and arranged sentences all on the same topic—paragraphing.

EXERCISE 1: IDENTIFYING PARAGRAPHS

Only one group links sentences in a clear arrangement to make a good paragraph. Which group is it, A or B?

PARAGRAPH ONE (from *A Monster Calls* by Patrick Ness)

Group A	Group B
(1) Conor could see raggedy teeth made of hard, knotted wood in the monster's open mouth, and he felt hot breath rushing up toward him. (2) It swung him out of his room and into the night, high above his backyard, holding him up against the circle of the moon, its fingers clenching so hard against Conor's ribs he could barely breathe. (3) The last thing Conor remembered was the monster's mouth roaring open to eat him alive. (4) The monster roared even louder and smashed an arm through Conor's window, shattering glass and wood and brick. (5) A huge, twisted, branch-wound hand grabbed Conor around the middle and lifted him off the floor.	(1) The monster roared even louder and smashed an arm through Conor's window, shattering glass and wood and brick. (2) A huge, twisted, branch-wound hand grabbed Conor around the middle and lifted him off the floor. (3) It swung him out of his room and into the night, high above his backyard, holding him up against the circle of the moon, its fingers clenching so hard against Conor's ribs he could barely breathe. (4) Conor could see raggedy teeth made of hard, knotted wood in the monster's open mouth, and he felt hot breath rushing up toward him. (5) The last thing Conor remembered was the monster's mouth roaring open to eat him alive.

PARAGRAPH TWO (from *The Giver* by Lois Lowry)

Group A	Group B
(1) He had seen it both times. (2) Squinting toward the sky, he had seen the sleek jet, almost a blur at its high speed, go past, and a second later heard the blast of sound that followed. (3) Frightened meant that deep, sickening feeling of something terrible about to happen. (4) Then one more time, a moment later, from the opposite direction, came the same plane. (5) Frightened was the way he had felt a year ago when an unidentified aircraft had overflown the community twice. (6) Jonas was beginning to be frightened.	(1) Jonas was beginning to be frightened. (2) Frightened meant that deep, sickening feeling of something terrible about to happen. (3) Frightened was the way he had felt a year ago when an unidentified aircraft had overflown the community twice. (4) He had seen it both times. (5) Squinting toward the sky, he had seen the sleek jet, almost a blur at its high speed, go past, and a second later heard the blast of sound that followed. (6) Then one more time, a moment later, from the opposite direction, came the same plane.

PARAGRAPH THREE (from *The Phantom Tollbooth* by Norton Juster)

Group A	Group B
(1) Without stopping or looking up, Milo dashed past the buildings and busy shops that lined the street, and, in a few minutes, reached home, dashing through the lobby, hopping onto the elevator and off again, opening the apartment door, rushing into his room, flopping dejectedly into a chair, and grumbling softly. (2) He looked glumly at all the things he owned, including the books that were too much trouble to read, the tools he'd never learned to use, the small electric automobile he hadn't driven in months, and the hundreds of other games and toys, and bats and balls, and bits and pieces, all scattered around him. (3) Then, to one side of the room, just next to the stereo, he noticed something he had never seen before, something larger than almost any other big package that he'd ever seen.	(1) Then, to one side of the room, just next to the stereo, he noticed something he had never seen before, something larger than almost any other big package that he'd ever seen. (2) He looked glumly at all the things he owned, including the books that were too much trouble to read, the tools he'd never learned to use, the small electric automobile he hadn't driven in months, and the hundreds of other games and toys, and bats and balls, and bits and pieces, all scattered around him. (3) Without stopping or looking up, Milo dashed past the buildings and busy shops that lined the street, and, in a few minutes, reached home, dashing through the lobby, hopping onto the elevator and off again, opening the apartment door, rushing into his room, flopping dejectedly into a chair, and grumbling softly.

PARAGRAPH FOUR (from *The False Prince* by Jennifer A. Nielsen)

Group A	Group B
(1) I raced away from the market with a stolen roast of meat tucked under my arm. (2) It was very difficult to hold a chunk of meat while running because it was more slippery than I'd anticipated. (3) If the butcher didn't catch me with his cleaver first, and literally cut off my future plans, I vowed to remember to get the meat wrapped next time, and then steal it. (4) He was only a few paces behind now, chasing me at a better speed than I'd have expected for a man of his weight. (5) He yelled loudly in his native language, one I didn't recognize. (6) He was originally from one of the far countries, undoubtedly a country where killing a meat thief was allowed. (7) It was this sort of thought that encouraged me to run faster.	(1) It was this sort of thought that encouraged me to run faster. (2) He yelled loudly in his native language, one I didn't recognize. (3) It was very difficult to hold a chunk of meat while running because it was more slippery than I'd anticipated. (4) He was originally from one of the far countries, undoubtedly a country where killing a meat thief was allowed. (5) I raced away from the market with a stolen roast of meat tucked under my arm. (6) If the butcher didn't catch me with his cleaver first, and literally cut off my future plans, I vowed to remember to get the meat wrapped next time, and then steal it. (7) He was only a few paces behind now, chasing me at a better speed than I'd have expected for a man of his weight.

PARAGRAPH FIVE (from *39 Clues* by Peter Lerangis)

Group A	Group B
(1) They must have wanted some other nerdy kid with a plaid shirt. (2) His head banged against a row of metal shelves. (3) In all his eleven years, Atticus Rosenbloom never imagined he'd die on a bed of fresh rolls and sticky buns. (4) He jerked his body left and right, trying to loosen the ropes around his wrists. (5) This had to be a mistake. (6) Breads and pastries cascaded to the floor, their sweet yeasty smell seeming to mock him. (7) He never had imagined being tied up, shoved into a sack.	(1) In all his eleven years, Atticus Rosenbloom never imagined he'd die on a bed of fresh rolls and sticky buns. (2) He never had imagined being tied up, shoved into a sack. (3) This had to be a mistake. (4) They must have wanted some other nerdy kid with a plaid shirt. (5) He jerked his body left and right, trying to loosen the ropes around his wrists. (6) His head banged against a row of metal shelves. (7) Breads and pastries cascaded to the floor, their sweet yeasty smell seeming to mock him.

EXERCISE 2: FINDING THE MISSING LINK

Underneath the paragraph are three sentences. Identify the only sentence that links well with the rest of the paragraph in both what it says (*content*) and how it says it (*style*). Then identify the sentence that links poorly in content, and the sentence that links poorly in style.

USE THESE LETTERS FOR YOUR ANSWERS

A = sentence that links well with rest of the paragraph

B = sentence that links poorly because of its **content**

C = sentence that links poorly because of its **style**

**PARAGRAPH ONE (from *Finn Flanagan
and the Fledglings* by Kip Taylor)**

The angel spreads her arms, and a pair of enormous wings, fanning out at least four feet on either side, cascade from her shoulders to the floor, each feather pristine white. **FIND THE MISSING LINK.** A yellow circle glows above her head. It's her sapphire-blue eyes that finally penetrate my dense brain. She is the one who caught me as I fell from the mouth of the monster.

1. A stranger approached the group and asked directions to the planet.

2. The light from her radiant presence is terrific.

3. Bright pink light surges from her body and pulses over us.

PARAGRAPH TWO (from *Whittington* by Alan Armstrong)

The cat was the color of old metal, broad-faced with thick whiskers and dark lines that ran from his nose to his forehead and down his back and sides. His coat was rumpled and slack. His paws were black, his tail thick and ringed with black circles. **FIND THE MISSING LINK.** When he stood or sat, he rocked slightly from side to side like a punch-drunk fighter. He was stiff and walked low to the ground. His left ear hung down like a loose flap. He wasn't old, but he looked beaten up.

4. The tail was really amazing when it moved.

5. After the dog barked at the cat, the cat ran away.

6. It swelled out at the end like a fox's brush.

PARAGRAPH THREE (from *A Monster Calls* by Patrick Ness)

FIND THE MISSING LINK. Other branches twisted around one another, always creaking, always groaning, until they formed two long arms and a second leg to set down beside the main trunk. The rest of the tree gathered itself into a spine and then a torso, the thin, needle-like leaves weaving together to make a green, furry skin that moved and breathed as if there were muscles and lungs underneath. Already taller than Conor's window, the monster grew wider as it brought itself together, filling out to a powerful shape, one that looked somehow strong, somehow mighty. It stared at Conor the whole time, and he could hear the loud, windy breathing from its mouth. It set its giant hands on either side of his window, lowering its head until its huge eyes filled the frame, holding Conor with its glare.

7. Along the driveway were many trees standing tall like soldiers at attention.

8. Conor saw the tree branches make a face with a mouth, a nose, and eyes.

9. As Conor watched, the uppermost branches of the tree gathered themselves into a great and terrible face, shimmering into a mouth and nose and even eyes, peering back at him.

PARAGRAPH FOUR (from *A Wrinkle in Time* by Madeleine L'Engle)

In the kitchen, a light was already on, and Charles Wallace was sitting at the table drinking milk and eating bread and jam. He looked very small and vulnerable sitting there alone in the big old-fashioned kitchen, a blond little boy in faded blue flannel pajamas, his feet swinging a good six inches above the floor. **FIND THE MISSING LINK.** Fortinbras had arrived on their doorstep, a half-grown puppy, scrawny and abandoned, one winter night. He was part setter and part greyhound, and he had a slender, dark beauty that was all his own.

10. From under the table where he was lying at Charles Wallace's feet, hoping for a crumb or two, Fortinbras raised his slender dark head, and his tail thumped against the floor.

11. School had been cancelled that day because of the heavy snow clogging the roads in the small community.

12. Fortinbras was under the table and wagged his tail and hoped for a crumb.

PARAGRAPH FIVE (from *All American* by John R. Tunis)

From the stands you saw the ball carrier, blotted out by a mass of tacklers, while some player on the ground held one shoe. He was almost down. Suddenly, without warning, as if by magic, he shot from that mass of arms and legs and bodies and headguards and torn jerseys. He was free again. Someone slapped at him and missed. Someone else grabbed out, caught his headguard and ripped it off. His blonde hair shone in the autumn sunshine. He picked up speed, outraced one open-mouthed, groping enemy at his elbow, and reversing his field cut across in a kind of sweeping motion. The whole pattern on the grass dissolved into a number of units, all chasing one man. Hands pawed at him, reached for him, struck at his poised body, jumped at his head and shoulders. He whirled completely around, side-stepped a burly figure, slapped off another, when someone jarred his body and upset his stride. The blonde head stumbled forward. The body tripped and almost fell. His face was close to the ground, yet his feet kept moving like pinwheels. Once again he appeared to be finished. **FIND THE MISSING LINK.** His body control perfect, he swung back instinctively into open territory almost without raising his head. From behind a huge shape came after him, fast, faster. Ronald glanced back, his mouth wide open in fatigue. Just ahead was the goal. He saw the pursuer gaining slowly. The body came through the air and leaped for him. Ronald stepped deftly aside at the right moment. The tackler rolled over and over harmlessly on the turf.

13. The sky opened and there was a deluge of pounding rain.

14. Somehow he kept in motion, kept on running, stumbling, head down, until he managed to recover balance.

15. He looks like he was in a drunken stupor.

EXERCISE 3: MATCHING

Each paragraph is missing a sentence. It might be the preview (topic) sentence, or one of the linking sentences. Match the sentence with its paragraph.

Paragraphs	Missing Sentences
1. My hair stands on end and the lightning strikes the tree. A flash of white runs up the wire, and for just a moment, the dome bursts into a dazzling blue light. **(MISSING SENTENCE)** Suzanne Collins, *Catching Fire*	**a.** Each time I picked myself up and rushed on, panting, crying.
2. I rushed off toward the forest. Barely aware of the earth beneath my feet or the roof of trees above, I paid no mind into what I ran, or that my sole garment, a gray wool tunic, tore on brambles and bushes. Nor did I care that my leather shoes, catching roots or stones, kept tripping me, causing me to fall. **(MISSING SENTENCE)** Deeper and deeper into the ancient woods I went, past thick bracken and stately oaks, until I tripped and fell again. Avi, *Crispin: The Cross of Lead*	**b.** The pilot sat large, his hands lightly on the wheel, feet on the rudder pedals.

3. (MISSING SENTENCE) He seemed more a machine than a man, an extension of the plane. On the dashboard in front of him Brian saw dials, switches, meters, knobs, levers, cranks, lights, handles that were wiggling and flickering, all indicating nothing that he understood and the pilot seemed the same way: part of the plane, not human.

Gary Paulsen, *Hatchet*

4. The first thing you would notice about our island, I think, is the wind. **(MISSING SENTENCE)** All the winds except the one from the south are strong. Because of them, the hills are polished smooth, and the trees are small and twisted, even in the canyon that runs down to Coral Cover.

Scott O'Dell, *Island of the Blue Dolphins*

5. The pen didn't look like much, just a regular cheap ballpoint, but when Percy uncapped it, it grew into a glowing bronze sword. The blade balanced perfectly. The leather grip fit his hand like it had been custom designed for him. **(MISSING SENTENCE)**

Rick Riordan, *The Son of Neptune*

c. It blows almost every day, sometimes from the northwest and sometimes from the east, once in a long while out of the south.

d. I'm thrown backward to the ground, body useless, paralyzed, eyes frozen wide, as feathery bits of matter rain down on me.

e. Etched along the guard was an ancient word Percy somehow understood: *Riptide*.

EXERCISE 4: CREATING

Read each paragraph slowly several times to learn its topic. Create a new sentence that links to that topic. Build your sentence like an author builds sentences so yours blends into the paragraph.

1. Dan loved collecting things. He collected baseball cards, autographs of famous outlaws, Civil War weapons, rare coins. **(YOUR SENTENCE)** At the moment, what he liked collecting best were charcoal rubbings of tombstones. He has some awesome ones back at the apartment.

    Rick Riordan, *A Maze of Bones*

2. Alone in Room 215 of the hotel and unaware that he was being watched, the boy began to explore. He got down on his hands and knees and looked under the bed. He leaned out the open window as far as he could and greedily inhaled deep breaths of pine-scented air. **(YOUR SENTENCE)** Under the window he discovered a knothole in the pine wall down by the floor and, squatting, poked his finger into the hole. When he felt nothing inside, he lost interest.

    Beverly Cleary, *The Mouse and the Motorcycle*

3. **(YOUR SENTENCE)** A little dog with skinny legs was between his feet. Beside them was a tin can with a few coins in it. Ben reached into his pocket, bent down, and added all of his change. The city seemed to swirl and explode around them, and even though New York City had to be the loudest place on earth, the man and his dog slept through it.

    Brian Selznick, *Wonderstruck*

4. Way out at the end of a tiny little town was an overgrown garden, and in the garden was an old house, and in the house lived Pippi

Longstocking. She was nine years old, and she lived there all alone. She had no mother and no father. **(YOUR SENTENCE)**

Astrid Lindgren, *Pippi Longstocking*

5. **(YOUR SENTENCE)** The eyes were greenish and narrow and the eyebrow line above them ran straight across the bridge of the nose, giving the effect of a monkey rather than a man. One cheek was marked with a buttonlike scar, the scar of the button plague so common in the lands. The ears were low set and ugly. The mouth looked like the slit that boys make in the pumpkins they carry on Halloween. Above the mouth was a cropped mustache which hung down at the ends and straggled into a scanty beard.

Eric P. Kelly, *The Trumpeter of Krakow*

SUMMARY: WHAT'S A PARAGRAPH?

A paragraph is a series of linked sentences on the same topic. It's like a sentence, only longer. A sentence has a topic (*its subject*) and a comment about that topic (*its predicate*).

EXAMPLE

A red bolt flashed from his palm toward the elven lady and illuminated the trees with a bloody light.

Sentence Topic: The subject is *a red bolt*

Comment About Topic: The predicate tells two things the red bolt did (*flashed from his palm toward the elven lady and illuminated the trees with a bloody light*).

A paragraph also has a topic and comments about that topic, but needs more comments (sentences) to tell about that topic. In the example paragraph, from a fantasy story, the topic is an attempt to kill an elven lady. That topic is in the first sentence of the paragraph, often called a *preview sentence* or *topic sentence*. Each sentence after the first sentence links to that topic by telling new information.

EXAMPLE

(1) A red bolt flashed from his palm toward the elven lady and illuminated the trees with a bloody light. (2) It struck her steed, and the horse toppled with a high-pitched squeal, plowing into the ground chest-first. (3) She leapt off the animal with inhuman speed, landed lightly, glancing back for her guards.

Christopher Paolini, *Eragon*

Paragraph Topic: *attempt to kill an elven lady*

Comments About Topic:

The first sentence tells what was used in the attempt to kill her (*a red bolt*).

The second sentence tells what the bolt did (*toppled the lady's horse*).

The third sentence tells what happened to the lady (*survived the attempt*).

PARAGRAPH WORKOUT

- You've learned that a paragraph sometimes starts with a preview (topic) sentence, followed by sentences that link to it.

- In this exercise, an author provides a preview sentence, and, as that author's partner, you compose at least five sentences that link to it.

- Before you start, look back at how the authors' sentences in the paragraphs in exercises in this section are built. Build your sentences the way authors build theirs.

- After revising your paragraph, give it a title that sums it up.

PREVIEW (TOPIC) SENTENCES

1. Earth, our little blue and green planet, the one with the fluffy white clouds and all, is under attack.

   K. A. Applegate, *Animorphs: The Underground*

2. Mr. President was a well-fed cat who always wore a collar with his name and number on a tag.

   Esther Averill, *Jenny and the Cat Club*

3. Coraline dreamed of black shapes that slid from place to place, avoiding the light, little black shapes with little red eyes and sharp yellow teeth.

   Neil Gaiman, *Coraline*

4. Unable to find a bat for a four-year-old, my father bought a standard-size Louisville Slugger and then took a saw to it.

   Jerry Spinelli, *Knots in My Yo-Yo String*

5. More than anyone, he had cause to fear the king.

   Megan Whalen Turner, *The King of Atollia*

6. Good thing the plane had seat belts and we'd been strapped in tight before takeoff.

   Rita Williams-Garcia, *One Crazy Summer*

7. That afternoon the Kid felt he learned as much baseball sitting beside Dave Leonard as he had learned all season.

    John R. Tunis, *World Series*

8. As she headed down the hall to her next class, Geraldine remembered that she hadn't done the homework for English.

    Toni Cade Bambara, "Geraldine Moore the Poet"

9. In a minute, the faded red double doors of the lunchroom swung open, and Sistine Bailey came marching through them, her head held high.

    Kate DiCamillo, *The Tiger Rising*

10. Terrified, she heard a lot of creaking.

    Louise Fitzhugh, *Harriet the Spy*

REVIEW

A paragraph is a container for linked sentences on the same topic. Each linked sentence says more about the paragraph's topic.

PREVIEW

Since paragraphs are made up of sentences, you'll learn the basics required for every sentence: a subject and a predicate.

BASIC SENTENCE PARTS

Some things go together: burgers and fries, school and, yes, homework, and sentences and paragraphs. You almost can't have one without the other. *Paragraphs for Elementary School: A Sentence-Composing Approach* is all about writing better sentences to build better paragraphs. For every sentence, though, you need two things: a subject and a predicate.

A sentence tells people something about a topic. The topic is called a *subject*. The comment about the topic is called a *predicate*. Subjects are topics, and predicates are comments about them.

THESE ARE JUST TOPICS, NOT SENTENCES

1. the kids in Room 207

2. the tiny Indian

3. Harry the Dirty Dog

4. playing jokes on people

5. to get his feet wet in such a cold temperature

6. smoke and flames

7. the large woman

8. whoever had worn those sneakers

9. whatever whispered in my ear

10. what my world hasn't got

THESE ARE JUST COMMENTS, NOT SENTENCES

1. were misbehaving again

2. walked around the little tepee three times slowly

3. felt tired and hungry

4. didn't have to stop because you got grown

5. meant trouble and danger

6. were pouring out of the blackened spaces where the windows had been

7. turned around and kicked him right square in his blue-jeaned sitter

8. had a bad case of foot odor

9. made my eyes pop open

10. is not worth having

The two lists above are not sentences. They are only topics and comments. A sentence is a group of words with a topic (called a "subject") and a comment about that topic (called a "predicate"). Below, the ten topics and ten comments about those topics are linked to make ten complete sentences, each with a subject and a predicate—the two sentence parts every sentence needs.

Subject (topic)	Predicate (comment about the topic)
1. The kids in Room 207	were misbehaving again. Harry Allard, *Miss Nelson Is Missing!*
2. The tiny Indian	walked around the little tepee three times slowly. Lynne Reid Banks, *The Indian in the Cupboard*
3. Harry the Dirty Dog	felt tired and hungry. Gene Zion, *"Harry the Dirty Dog"*
4. Playing jokes on people	didn't have to stop because you got grown. Olive Ann Burns, *Cold Sassy Tree*
5. To get his feet wet in such a cold temperature	meant trouble and danger. Jack London, *"To Build a Fire"*

6. Smoke and flames	were pouring out of the blackened spaces where the windows had been. Franklin W. Dixon, *The Secret of the Old Mill*
7. The large woman	turned around and kicked him right square in his blue-jeaned sitter. Langston Hughes, *"Thank You, M'am"*
8. Whoever had worn those sneakers	had a bad case of foot odor. Louis Sachar, *Holes*
9. Whatever whispered in my ear	made my eyes pop open. Rosa Guy, *Edith Jackson*
10. What my world hasn't got	is not worth having. Kenneth Grahame, *The Wind in the Willows*

EXERCISE 1: MATCHING

Match the subject with its predicate to make a sentence. Write out each sentence.

8/23/23

Subjects	Predicates
1. A board ^ Thomas Rockwell, *How to Eat Fried Worms*	**a.** had ten minutes left to get on the train to Hogwarts
2. A deeper fog ^ Barbara Brooks Wallace, *Peppermints in the Parlor*	**b.** trotted frantically through the mounds of men, tossing its head, whinnying in panic
3. A whirl of bats frightened from slumber by their smoking torches ^ J. R. R. Tolkien, *The Hobbit*	**c.** had begun to creep stealthily up from the sea, spreading over San Francisco to dim the lights of its buildings and to turn them into monstrous shadows
4. According to the large clock over the arrival board, he ^ J. K. Rowling, *Harry Potter and the Sorcerer's Stone*	**d.** creaked on the stairs
5. A wild-eyed horse, its bridle torn and dangling, ^ . Lois Lowry, *The Giver*	**e.** flurried over the dwarves

Sometimes sentences have more than one subject. Those sentences say something about more than one topic.

8/23/23 **EXAMPLES**

1. **The four children** and **the Dwarf** went down to the water's edge to push off the boat with some difficulty. (*two subjects with same predicate*)

   C. S. Lewis, *Prince Caspian*

2. **Every garage, every little-used road, every patch of woods** was thoroughly investigated. (*three subjects with same predicate*)

   Franklin W. Dixon, *The Tower Treasure*

3. The next day, **Pip**, **Flitter**, **Flap**, and **Stellaluna** went flying far from home. (*four subjects with same predicate*)

   Janell Cannon, *Stellaluna*

Sometimes sentences have more than one predicate. Those sentences say more than one thing about the subject.

8/23/23 **EXAMPLES**

1. Ramona **scowled** and **slid down in her chair**. (*two predicates with one subject*)

   Beverly Cleary, *Ramona and Her Father*

2. He **felt something cold on his ankles** and **looked under the tablecloth** and **saw two more of the huge worms around his ankles**. (*three predicates with one subject*)

   Thomas Rockwell, *How to Eat Fried Worms*

3. The tiny Indian **walked around the little tepee three times slowly, went down on hands and knees, crawled in through the flap, came out again after a minute, tugged at the felt, stood**

back to look at the poles, and **gave a fairly satisfied grunt**. (*seven predicates with one subject*)

> Lynne Reid Banks, *The Indian in the Cupboard*

Sometimes sentences have more than one subject *and* more than one predicate. Those sentences say more than one thing about more than one topic. **Directions:** Read the examples and tell the subjects and predicates.

EXAMPLES

1. Frank and Joe Hardy clutched the grips of their motorcycles and stared in horror at the oncoming car. (*two subjects and two predicates*)

   > Franklin W. Dixon, *The Tower Treasure*

2. Alan and Tom and Joe leaned on their shovels under a tree in the apple orchard and watched the worms squirming on a flat rock. (*three subjects and two predicates*)

   > Thomas Rockwell, *How to Eat Fried Worms*

3. Hastily, he and I tugged on the well rope, pulled up the water tube, and poured the water into the bucket. (*two subjects and three predicates*)

   > Mildred D. Taylor, *Roll of Thunder, Hear My Cry*

EXERCISE 2: CREATING SUBJECTS AND PREDICATES

Directions: At each caret mark, add a <u>subject</u> that links to the rest of the author's sentence.

1. ^ were still glowing in the fireplace, turning all the armchairs into hunched black shadows.

   > J. K. Rowling, *Harry Potter and the Sorcerer's Stone*

2. Among all Arawn's deeds, ^ is one of the cruelest.

   > Lloyd Alexander, *The Book of Three*

3. Always meticulously neat, ^ never allowed dirt or tears or stains to mar anything he owned.

    Mildred D. Taylor, *Roll of Thunder, Hear My Cry*

4. After Jim had pulled some tangled pine branches away from the convertible, ^ and ^ were able to lift the trunk.

    Carolyn Keene, *The Bungalow Mystery*

5. All at once, ^ rolled down one of the Big Friendly Giant's cheeks and fell with a splash on the floor.

    Roald Dahl, *The BFG*

Directions: At each caret mark, complete the <u>predicate</u> by telling other actions the subject did.

6. A burning limb fell into the pit, struck the water, ^ , and ^ .

    Jean Craighead George, *The Fire Bug Connection*

7. Frank picked up the costume, ^ , and ^ .

    Franklin W. Dixon, *The Tower Treasure*

8. Suddenly, a slim white cat sped through the grass, ^ , and ^ .

    Esther Averill, *Jenny and the Cat Club*

9. Justin was out with a mighty leap, hit the floor with a thump, ^ , and ^ , disappearing from my view, heading toward the end of the room.

    Robert C. O'Brien, *Mrs. Frisby and the Rats of NIMH*

10. The cats bit and scratched and ^ and ^ .

    Wanda Gag, "Millions of Cats"

Directions: These sentences have missing <u>subjects and predicates</u>. Add them at the caret marks.

11. Together, Ramona and ^ unrolled the paper across the kitchen and ^ .

    Beverly Cleary, *Ramona and Her Father*

12. Mrs. Sasaki and ^ had scrubbed and ^ the house until it shone.

    Eleanor Coerr, *Sadako and the Thousand Paper Cranes*

13. ^ reached the unicorn, lowered its head over the wound in the animal's side, and ^ .

    J. K. Rowling, *Harry Potter and the Sorcerer's Stone*

14. Somewhere beyond the sink-hole, past the magnolia, under the live oaks, a boy and ^ ran side by side, and ^ .

    Marjorie Kinnan Rawlings, *The Yearling*

15. ^ grabbed ink bottles and sprayed the class with them, ^ , ^ , ^ , ^ , and ^ .

    J. K. Rowling, *Harry Potter and the Chamber of Secrets*

SUMMARY

Every sentence must have at least one subject and at least one predicate.

Subject Facts	
1. Subjects can be at the very beginning of the sentence.	**Pa** was trying to hold up his end of the log to keep it from falling on Ma. Laura Ingalls Wilder, *Little House on the Prairie*
2. Subjects can even be at the end of a sentence.	On a hill above the valley was **a wood**. Roald Dahl, *Fantastic Mr. Fox*

3. Subjects can be long.	**Being bitten by a scorpion or even a rattlesnake** is not the worst thing that can happen to you. Louis Sachar, *Holes*
4. Subjects can be short.	**Harry** was a white dog with black spots who liked everything except getting a bath. Gene Zion, "Harry the Dirty Dog"
5. Subjects can do just one thing.	**Vasilissa** put the skull on the end of a stick. Post Wheeler, *Vasilissa the Beautiful*
6. Subjects can do more than one thing.	**Violet** wandered around the house, avoided Count Olaf all day, and cooked for his terrible friends every night. Lemony Snicket, *The Bad Beginning*
7. Sentences can have just one subject.	**The velveteen rabbit** grew to like sleeping in the boy's bed. Margery Williams, *The Velveteen Rabbit*
8. Sentences can have more than one subject.	**Cadavers** and **dead rats** and **frogs** had started appearing in his locker about three months earlier. Gary Paulsen, *The Time Hackers*
9. Sentences must have a subject—or they won't make sense! *Without a subject, we don't know who ate lunch together.*	(*no subject*) **?** ate lunch together around the side of the building. Louis Sachar, *There's a Boy in the Girl's Bathroom*

Predicate Facts	
1. Predicates usually come after the subject.	Stars, comets, planets **flashed across the sky.** Madeleine L'Engle, *A Wrinkle in Time*
2. Predicates sometimes come before the subject.	**On this mound among the grasses and the plants stood** Rontu. Scott O'Dell, *Island of the Blue Dolphins*

3. Predicates can be short.	To Harry's astonishment, Dumbledore **smiled.** J. K. Rowling, *Harry Potter and the Chamber of Secrets*
4. Predicates can be long.	Sam **caught a glimpse through an opening in the trees of the top of the green bank from which they had climbed.** J. R. R. Tolkien, *The Fellowship of the Ring*
5. Predicates can tell just one thing.	Dad **was standing at the sink with a coffee filter in his hand.** Laurel Snyder, *Bigger Than a Bread Box*
6. Predicates can tell more than one thing.	I **unhooked the wire, pushed the fence open, and led Shiloh to the stream for a drink after filling the pie pan with fresh water.** Phyllis Reynolds Naylor, *Shiloh*
7. Sentences must have predicates—or they won't make sense!	Soundlessly, Nancy **?** (*no predicate*) Carolyn Keene, *The Bungalow Mystery* *Without a predicate, we don't know what Nancy did soundlessly.*

PARAGRAPH WORKOUT

PART ONE

In the paragraph below, *subjects* have been removed at the caret mark (^). Create a subject to link to the predicate, and insert it at the mark. Vary the length of your subjects. Make some short, some medium, some long.

This paragraph describes a painful procedure performed by a doctor on a boy named Ender.

(1) The ^ was twisting something at the back of Ender's head.

(2) Suddenly a ^ stabbed through him like a needle from his neck to his

groin. (3) ^ felt his back spasm. (4) His ^ arched violently backward. (5) His ^ struck the bed. (6) ^ could feel his legs thrashing. (7) His ^ were clenching each other, wringing each other so tightly that they ached.

Orson Scott Card, *Ender's Game*

PART TWO

In the paragraph below, *predicates* have been removed at the caret mark (^). Create a predicate to link to the subject, and insert it at the mark. Vary the length of your predicates. Make some short, some medium, some long.

This paragraph describes how a young girl named Fern cares for her pet baby pig named Wilbur.

(1) Fern loved Wilbur more than anything. (2) She ^ . (3) Every morning, when she got up, she ^ . (4) Every afternoon, when the school bus stopped in front of her house, she ^ . (5) She ^ . (6) Fern's mother ^ . (7) Wilbur loved his milk. (8) He ^ . (9) He ^ .

E. B. White, *Charlotte's Web*

PART THREE

In the paragraph below, some *sentences* have been removed. Since sentences are made up of subjects and predicates, here you will add both. Create a sentence to link to the rest of the paragraph to provide the kind of information suggested. Vary the length and kind of the sentences you create.

This paragraph describes a young, kind, beautiful teacher adored by her students.

(1) Their teacher was called Miss Honey, and she could not have been more than twenty-three or twenty-four. (2) *Describe her face, eyes, and hair.* (3) *Describe her delicate body.* (4) *Describe her personality and its*

affect on her elementary school students. (5) Describe her understanding of the needs of her students.

Roald Dahl, *Matilda*

REVIEW

A sentence tells something about a topic. The topic is called a *subject*. The comment about the topic is called a *predicate*. Subjects and predicates come in many different shapes and sizes.

PREVIEW

Although every sentence needs a subject and a predicate, the best sentences have something more. They have additional sentence parts that add detail and dazzle. They are called sentence-composing tools because you can use them to build better sentences, and therefore better paragraphs.

SENTENCE-COMPOSING TOOLS

What makes the best hamburger? First, you'll need two basics: bread and meat. Then you want more: maybe cheese, catsup or mustard, onions, tomato, lettuce, pickles, and so forth. Add-ons make it tastier, and the best.

What makes the best sentence? First, you'll need two basics: a subject and a predicate. For best sentences, add-ons to a subject and a predicate make your sentences more "tasty" for readers. The add-ons are built by sentence-composing tools like ones authors use.

Learning tools to build "best sentences" for your paragraphs is the purpose of this worktext. *Tools are sentence parts added to a sentence to provide information beyond the subject and predicate.* Those tools help you add details and dazzle to your sentences and paragraphs.

Following are pairs of sentences. The first sentence is just a subject and predicate, without tools. The second sentence, with tools, says more and is more interesting. That sentence is the one the author wrote.

EXERCISE 1: TOOL TALK

Discuss with a partner what additional information the tools give the reader.

EXAMPLE

a. He was seated upon a throne.

b. **Clad in royal purple and ermine**, he was seated upon a throne, **which was at the same time both simple and majestic**.

Antoine de Saint-Exupéry, *The Little Prince*

SAMPLE TOOL TALK

The tool at the beginning of the sentence tells readers what color his clothes were (*purple*) and what they were made of (*ermine*). The tool at the end of the sentence describes the throne as a mix of fancy and simple styles (*simple and majestic*).

1a. Joe was a small boy.

1b. Joe was a small boy, **with dark hair and a long nose and big brown eyes**.

Thomas Rockwell, How to Eat Fried Worms

2a. I turned my attention to the book.

2b. **After my delicious dinner**, I turned my attention to the book, **still lying open on the floor**.

Deborah and James Howe, Bunnicula: A Rabbit-Tale of Mystery

3a. The great spider came from behind him and came at him.

3b. The great spider, **who had been busy tying him up while he dozed**, came from behind him and came at him.

J. R. R. Tolkien, The Hobbit

4a. It was not dark on the green lawn.

4b. It was not dark on the green lawn, **for instantly the eyes of all the skulls on the wall were lighted up and shone till the place was bright as day**.

Post Wheeler, Vasilissa the Beautiful

5a. Big Ma stepped back.

5b. Big Ma, **standing behind me**, stepped back, **pulling me with her**.

Mildred D. Taylor, Roll of Thunder, Hear My Cry

6a. The snake slithered straight toward Justin and raised itself again.

6b. Enraged, hissing furiously, the snake slithered straight toward Justin and raised itself again, **fangs exposed, poised to strike.**

J. K. Rowling, Harry Potter and the Chamber of Secrets

7a. A human brain was preserved in formaldehyde.

7b. In the lab at school, a human brain was preserved in formaldehyde, **which the seniors preparing for college had to take out and look at and study.**

Madeleine L'Engle, A Wrinkle in Time

8a. She had an almost overwhelming desire to look around.

8b. Suddenly, she had an almost overwhelming desire to look around, **to see what was behind the other doors and down the other corridors.**

Robert C. O'Brien, Mrs. Frisby and the Rats of NIMH

9a. The children's feet felt hot and heavy.

9b. The children's feet, **after the change from the cool water,** felt hot and heavy.

C. S. Lewis, Prince Caspian

10a. Every kind of pushcart was represented.

10b. Every kind of pushcart was represented, **including hot dogs and sauerkraut, roast chestnuts, old clothes, ice and coal, ices and ice cream sticks, fruit and vegetables, used cartons, shoelaces and combs, pretzels, dancing dolls, and nylon stockings.**

Jean Merrill, The Pushcart War

Questions: What two sentence parts cannot be removed without destroying the sentence? What sentence parts can be removed?

Answers: The subject and the predicate. Take out either, and the sentence is destroyed. Tools can be removed, but nobody wants to remove them because they're often the best parts of the sentence, adding detail and dazzle!

Look back at the ten sentences with tools. Which have tools at the beginning of the sentence? Which have tools in the middle? Which have tools at the end? Which have tools in more than one place? You can use sentence-composing tools almost anywhere within a sentence.

EXERCISE 2: IDENTIFYING SENTENCE PARTS

In each list below, one sentence part is the subject of the sentence, and one is the predicate. The rest are tools adding more details. Tell whether each sentence part is a *subject*, a *predicate*, or a *tool*.

Reminder: A *subject* is a topic. A *predicate* is a comment about the topic. A tool is a sentence part telling more information. For good sentences, subjects and predicates are certainly required, and tools are definitely desired.

EXAMPLE

   a. Taken by surprise and overwhelmed by sheer numbers, *(tool)*

   b. the Peacekeepers *(subject)*

   c. were initially overcome by the crowds. *(predicate)*

AUTHOR'S SENTENCE

Taken by surprise and overwhelmed by sheer numbers, the Peacekeepers were initially overcome by the crowds.

Suzanne Collins, *Catching Fire*

1a. A large woman

1b. came out from the back room,

1c. her hair in a frazzled bun.

Clare Vanderpool, *Moon Over Manifest*

2a. To keep from wobbling,

2b. Lice Peeking

2c. braced himself with both arms in the doorway.

Carl Hiaasen, *Flush*

3a. After breaking a telephone conversation in an abrupt manner,

3b. the person

3c. called back as soon as possible to explain what had happened.

Carolyn Keene, *The Bungalow Mystery*

4a. A thin spider web of sweat

4b. draped itself over his forehead,

4c. spreading into his hair.

Jacqueline Davies, *The Lemonade War*

5a. He

5b. was white and shaking,

5c. his mouth opening and shutting without words.

Leslie Morris, "Three Shots for Charlie Beston"

6a. Templeton,

6b. asleep in the straw,

6c. heard the commotion and awoke.

E. B. White, *Charlotte's Web*

7a. Lost in his studies,

7b. Oppenheimer

7c. paid little attention to the outside world.

Steve Sheinkin, Bomb

8a. Faintly over the rain,

8b. Grant

8c. heard the sound of a little girl screaming.

Michael Crichton, Jurassic Park

9a. With rattlesnake speed,

9b. Maniac Magee

9c. snatched the book back.

Jerry Spinelli, Maniac Magee

10a. To reassure herself,

10b. Emily

10c. reached inside her green velveteen coat, pulled out the gold locket that hung from a chain around her neck, and opened the clasp.

Barbara Brooks Wallace, Peppermints in the Parlor

Note: *Sentences 11–15 have two or more tools.*

11a. Until a few months ago,

11b. I

11c. was a boarding student at Yancy Academy,

11d. a private school for troubled kids in upstate New York.

Rick Riordan, The Lightning Thief

12a. Trying to appear something less than frantic under the searching scrutiny of his father,

12b. he

12c. checked his safety belt buckle with elaborate coolness,

12d. rubbing at an imaginary windshield spot with a gloved hand.

Gene Olson, The Roaring Road

13a. Trembling,

13b. the two girls

13c. followed him,

13d. brushing past the two remaining officers in the doorway,

13e. to the living room.

Lois Lowry, Number the Stars

14a. Charles Wallace,

14b. in yellow footed pajamas,

14c. his fresh wounds band-aided,

14d. his small nose looking puffy and red,

14e. slept on the foot of Meg's big brass bed,

14f. his head pillowed on the shiny black bulk of the dog.

Madeleine L'Engle, A Wind in the Door

15a. Their path

15b. wound,

15c. in and out,

15d. through the scrub,

15e. around palmetto clumps,

15f. over trunks of fallen trees,

15g. under dwarf pines and oaks.

Lois Lenski, Strawberry Girl

EXERCISE 3: MATCHING

Match the subjects and predicates with the tools to build a more detailed sentence. *Write out each sentence.*

PART ONE

Each tool is at the <u>beginning</u> of the sentence.

Subjects and Predicates	Tools

1. ^ , the two girls groped their way among the other sleepers and crept out of the tent.
  C. S. Lewis, *The Lion, the Witch,*
  and the Wardrobe
	a. At the chicken coop

	b. Quick as lightning
2. ^ , Stuart noticed one boat that seemed to him finer and prouder than any other. E. B. White, *Stuart Little*	
	c. Very quietly
3. ^ , George ran out through the open door. Hans Augusto Rey, *Curious George*	
	d. Although he tried not to
4. ^ , Marty couldn't help flinging his arms up before his face. Murray Heyert, "The New Kid"	
	e. As he sat cross-legged on the wall that surrounds the pond to gaze out at the ships through his spyglass
5. ^ , Ida the hen was cackling excitedly among her chicks. Roger Duvoisin, "Petunia"	

PART TWO

Each tool is in the <u>middle</u> of the sentence.

Subjects and Predicates	Tools
6. Chester the cat, ^ , was rubbing against Mrs. Monroe's ankles and purring loudly. Deborah and James Howe, *Bunnicula: A Rabbit-Tale of Mystery*	**a.** after following the boys as far as the door of the school
7. Frank, ^ , carefully questioned Tony. Franklin W. Dixon, *The Secret of the Old Mill*	**b.** its ends tucked into his coat
8. A thick scarf, ^ , was crossed over his chest. Leslie Morris, "Three Shots for Charlie Beston"	**c.** eager for any possible lead
9. Henry's dog Ribsy, ^ , came trotting over to check the odors of the school's trash can. Beverly Cleary, *Ribsy*	**d.** who had also been named Fluffy for a short time
10. A navigational compass, ^ , is made from a small piece of magnetized metal and a simple pivot. Lemony Snicket, *The End*	**e.** as any good inventor knows

PART THREE

Each tool is at the <u>end</u> of the sentence.

Subjects and Predicates	Tools
11. Straight and true sailed the Wasp, ^ . E. B. White, *Stuart Little*	**a.** wild and tattered and hungry-looking
12. Out of the drain popped the little Tub Child, ^ . Pam Conrad, "The Tub People"	**b.** complaining that she wanted to stay up with the others, that she was grown-up enough, that she had never before seen a dead person in a closed-up box, that it wasn't fair
13. I looked out across the frozen glitter and saw a gray fox sitting on our fence, ^ . Bill and Vera Cleaver, *Where the Lilies Bloom*	**c.** wet and tired
14. Kirsti had gone to bed reluctantly, ^ . Lois Lowry, *Number the Stars*	**d.** exclaiming over her gold eyelashes, her pink underlip, her funny knobby knees, her short floppy tail, the furry insides of her ears.
15. They could have gazed at the pony forever, ^ . Marguerite Henry, *Misty of Chincoteague*	**e.** with Stuart at the helm

PART FOUR

These sentences have tools in two different places. Insert the two tools at the caret marks (^).

Subjects and Predicates	Tools
16. ^ , she had an almost overwhelming desire to look around, ^ . Robert C. O'Brien, *Mrs. Frisby and the Rats of NIMH*	**a.** Propped on her elbows with her chin in her fists / trying to catch his eye
17. ^ , she stared at the black wolf, ^ . Jean Craighead George, *Julie of the Wolves*	**b.** At night / under the stars
18. Dr. DeSoto, ^ , did very good work, ^ . William Steig, *Doctor DeSoto*	**c.** the dentist / so he had no end of patients
19. ^ , Harry saw that what had hold of him was marching on six immensely long, hairy legs, ^ . J. K. Rowling, *Harry Potter and the Chamber of Secrets*	**d.** Suddenly / to see what was behind the other doors and down the other corridors
20. ^ , they slept on the ground, ^ . Kate DiCamillo, *The Miraculous Journey of Edward Tulane*	**e.** Head hanging / the front two clutching him tightly below a pair of shining black pincers

EXERCISE 4: UNSCRAMBLING

Unscramble and arrange the sentence parts like the model. In the scrambled sentence, identify the *subject*, the *predicate*, and the *tools*.

EXAMPLE

Model: Before long, the chipmunk ran up, with cheeks bulging.

Randall Jarrell, *The Bat Poet*

SCRAMBLED SENTENCE PARTS

a. came flying (*predicate*)

b. the ball (*subject*)

c. with lightning speed (*tool*)

d. after that (*tool*)

Unscrambled Sentence: After that, the ball came flying, with lightning speed.

1. **Model:** The stallion tried to escape, charging against the chest board of his stall again and again.

   Marguerite Henry, *Misty of Chincoteague*

   a. pressing on the correct keys

   b. the students

   c. over and over

   d. of their keyboards

   e. learned to type

2. **Model:** Billy's father came into the kitchen, his tie loosened, and his jacket over his arm.

   Thomas Rockwell, *How to Eat Fried Worms*

   a. walked across the diamond

   b. his stare focusing

   c. and his glove on his hip

   d. the star pitcher

3. **Model:** As the door to the cupboard swung open, the tiny horse shied nervously, turning his face and pricking his ears so far forward they almost met over his forelock.

   Lynne Reid Banks, *The Indian in the Cupboard*

   a. the happy farmer

   b. and shaking his umbrella so fast that it almost fell from his hand

   c. closing the barn-door

   d. took shelter gratefully

   e. when the rain during the storm poured down

4. **Model:** As one of the phones began ringing, she stood up and walked out of the room, followed by Klaus, who was carrying Sunny.

   Lemony Snicket, *The Bad Beginning*

   a. looked up and swayed to the music

   b. who were imitating her

   c. the teacher

   d. followed by others

   e. after some of her students started singing

5. **Model:** As the carriage trundled toward a pair of magnificent wrought-iron gates, flanked with stone columns topped with winged boars, Harry saw two more towering, hooded dementors, standing guard on either side.

J. K. Rowling, *Harry Potter and the Prisoner of Azkaban*

a. heard one single, terrifying shriek

b. when the horse galloped within the mist around the castle's enormous fortress

c. Sir Neville

d. breaking silence like sudden thunder

e. surrounded by grey roads dotted with crumbling statues

Tool Facts	

1. Tools can be placed at the *beginning*, in the *middle*, or at the *end* of a sentence.	BEGINNING (*comma after the tool*)
	
	Inside the house, little jets of freezing air came rushing in through the sides of the windows and under the doors.
	
	    Roald Dahl, *Charlie and the Chocolate Factory*
	
	MIDDLE (*comma before and after the tool*)
	
	The other paw, **still tied up with Jessie's handkerchief,** was held off the ground.
	
	    Gertrude Chandler Warner, *The Boxcar Children*
	
	END (*comma before the tool*)
	
	Harry the dog fell asleep in his favorite place, **dreaming of how much fun it had been getting dirty**.
	
	    Gene Zion, "Harry the Dirty Dog"

2. A tool can be a word.	**WORD** **Wisely**, my mother did not try to dissuade me. Jean Craighead George, *My Side of the Mountain*
3. A tool can be a phrase. Phrases are groups of words without a subject and predicate.	**PHRASE** He moved around to the rear of the car and was rummaging in the back of the station wagon, **pulling at what looked like a bunch of junk to me.** Gary Paulsen, *The Monument*
4. A tool can be a dependent clause. *Clauses* are groups of words with a subject and predicate. A dependent clause is a sentence part of a complete sentence.	**CLAUSE** (dependent) **As <u>I</u> <u>lay stretched out</u>**, my puppies crawled all over me. Wilson Rawls, *Where the Red Fern Grows*
5. Sentences can have more than one tool of the same kind.	**MULTIPLE TOOLS** **WORDS** A shaft of sunlight, **warm** and **thin**, lay across his body. Marjorie Kinnan Rawlings, *The Yearling* **PHRASES** She noticed two small blackbirds nearby, **their beaks open, their feathers puffed up.** Susan Patron, *The Higher Power of Lucky* **CLAUSES** That face belonged to Phoebe Winterbottom, **who had a powerful imagination, who would become my friend, and who would have many peculiar things happen to her.** Sharon Creech, *Walk Two Moons*

6. Sentences can have more than one tool of different kinds, together or apart.	**MIXED TOOLS** TOOLS TOGETHER The only light in here came from the fireplace, **where a bright blaze of logs settled slightly** (*clause*), **sending a fountain of sparks up into the chimney** (*phrase*). <div align="right">Philip Pullman, *The Golden Compass*</div> TOOLS APART The fifth-grade boys, **bursting with new importance** (*phrase*), ordered the fourth graders around, **while the smaller boys tried to include themselves without being conspicuous.** (*clause*). <div align="right">Katherine Paterson, *Bridge to Terabithia*</div>
7. Tools can be short, medium, or long.	SHORT (*1–5 words*) Two boys, **each carrying a shovel**, were coming across the compound. <div align="right">Louis Sachar, *Holes*</div> MEDIUM (6–10 words) **When I was four and Cass was six**, she whacked me across the face with a plastic shovel at our neighborhood park. <div align="right">Sarah Dessen, *Dreamland*</div> LONG (*10+ words*) By the door lay another dog, **its brown eyes open and watchful in contrast to the peacefulness radiated by the other occupants of the room.** <div align="right">Sheila Burnford, *The Incredible Journey*</div>

PARAGRAPH WORKOUT

PART ONE

In the following paragraph, a character describes a strange and mysterious man. From the tools listed underneath the paragraph, find each missing tool and insert it at the caret (^). Copy the finished paragraph.

PARAGRAPH FOR THE TOOLS

(1) The second man I'd never seen before. (2) ^ , ^, he wore a hood attached to a flowing cape, ^ . (3) Gray hair reached his shoulders. (4) His blue over-tunic was long, quilted, and dark, ^ . (5) ^, I also saw the fine head of a horse. (6) I assumed it was the stranger's.

Avi, *Crispin: The Cross of Lead*

TOOLS (LISTED RANDOMLY)

with yellow clasps that gleamed in the torchlight

dressed like a gentleman

within the circle of light

with a face of older years

which hung down behind his legs

PART TWO

In the paragraph on the next page, a horse recalls pleasant experiences when it was a pony. Find the sentence in the paragraph where each tool belongs, and insert it at the caret (^). Copy the finished paragraph.

PARAGRAPH FOR THE TOOLS

(1) The first place that I can well remember was a large pleasant meadow, ^ . (2) Some shady trees leaned over it, and rushes and water-lilies grew at the deep end. (3) Over the hedge on one side, we looked into a plowed field. (4) ^ , we looked over a gate at our master's house, ^ . (5) At the top of the meadow was a grove of fir trees, and at the bottom a running brook, ^ . (6) ^ , I lived upon my mother's milk, as I could not eat grass. (7) In the daytime, I ran by her side. (8) At night, I lay down close by her. (9) ^ , we used to stand by the pond in the shade of the trees. (10) ^ , we had a nice warm shed near the grove.

Anna Sewell, *Black Beauty*

TOOLS (LISTED RANDOMLY)

when it was cold

while I was young

overhung by a steep bank

with a pond of clear water in it

when it was hot

which stood by the roadside

on the other side

PART THREE

In the paragraph on the next page, a young trumpeter is killed by an enemy's arrow. To strengthen the paragraph, create a tool to insert at each caret mark (^). Use tools of different lengths—some short, some medium, some long. Copy the finished paragraph.

PARAGRAPH FOR THE TOOLS

(1) An enemy below crouched to his bow and drew back the arrow ^ . (2) The string whirred. (3) ^ , the dark arrow flew straight for the mark. (4) The arrow pierced the breast of the young trumpeter ^ .
(5) The arrow quivered there a moment, and the song ceased. (6) ^ , the youth fell back against the supporting wall and blew one last glorious note. (7) The note began strongly, trembled, and then eased, ^ .

Eric P. Kelly, *The Trumpeter of Krakow*

REVIEW

Sentence-composing tools transform ordinary sentences into extraordinary sentences. Tools can make almost any sentence better. They can be anywhere in a sentence—the beginning, middle, or end.

PREVIEW

Authors use lots of those tools in the sentences in their paragraphs. You can, too. One way is by imitating the way their sentences are built. Sentences by authors can be blueprints for building your own sentences in similar ways.

CHUNKING SENTENCES

When you eat a hamburger, you don't swallow it whole. You eat it one chunk at a time. That way your body can digest it. When you read or write a sentence, you do it one chunk at a time. That way your mind can understand it. People read and write sentences one sentence part at a time. Each sentence part is a "chunk" of meaning in a sentence.

A good chunk makes sense by itself. A bad chunk doesn't. The sentences below are chunked, but only one column has good chunks. Read each chunk to the slash mark (/) and you'll be able to see the difference between bad chunks (*left column*) and good chunks (*right column*).

Bad Chunks	Good Chunks
1. As the / dragon charged, it released huge / clouds of hissing /steam through its nostrils.	As the dragon charged, / it released huge clouds / of hissing steam / through its nostrils. Broun, Heywood, "The Fifty-First Dragon"
2. Beetee, in / the moments that led up to his / victory in those / long-ago Hunger Games, watched the / others die.	Beetee, / in the moments / that led up to his victory / in those long-ago Hunger Games, / watched the others die. Suzanne Collins, *Mockingjay*
3. He tried to spit on / the boy, but it / trickled down his / chin, his tongue refusing to / obey him.	He tried / to spit on the boy, / but it trickled / down his chin, / his tongue refusing to obey him. Becca Fitzpatrick, *Hush, Hush*
4. Gabriel was / looking through the / windshield, his eyes a little / closed and tight, like he / was looking into the wind.	Gabriel was looking / through the windshield, / his eyes a little closed and tight, / like he was looking / into the wind. Joseph Krumgold, *. . . And Now Miguel*

5. At the / foot of one of the / trees, the boy's father, puzzled by the / footsteps, sat, the lantern still / burning by his side.	At the foot of one of the trees, / the boy's father, / puzzled by the footsteps, / sat, / the lantern still burning / by his side. William H. Armstrong, *Sounder*

EXERCISE 1: FINDING CHUNKS

Read each pair of sentences a chunk at a time. <u>Important</u>: Read out loud, and pause where each slash mark (/) occurs. If the reading doesn't make sense, then the chunks are wrong. They're bad chunks. If the reading does make sense, congratulations! You found the good chunks. Copy the sentence and slash marks that make sense because the sentence is divided into good chunks.

EXAMPLE

a. The / idea of cutting and sewing a / dress by / herself was novel and exciting.

b. The idea / of cutting and sewing a dress / by herself / was novel and exciting.

Elizabeth George Speare, *The Witch of Blackbird Pond*

CORRECT: **b**

1a. The diggers gathered about / the rim of the / pit, staring.

1b. The diggers gathered / about the rim of the pit, / staring.

Edmund Ware, "An Underground Episode"

2a. Rob's eyes, growing / accustomed to the bright / sunlight, took in details.

2b. Rob's eyes, / growing accustomed to the bright sunlight, / took in details.

John Christopher, The Guardians

3a. He was white and shaking, his / mouth opening and shutting without / words.

3b. He was white and shaking, / his mouth opening and shutting / without words.

Leslie Morris, "Three Shots for Charlie Beston"

4a. She set the little creature down, / and felt quite relieved / to see it trot away quietly / into the wood.

4b. She set the / little creature down, and felt quite relieved to / see it trot away quietly into / the wood.

Lewis Carroll, Alice's Adventures in Wonderland

5a. A thousand live / bats fluttered from the walls and ceiling while a thousand / more swooped over the tables in low / black clouds.

5b. A thousand live bats / fluttered from the walls and ceiling / while a thousand more swooped over the tables / in low black clouds.

J. K. Rowling, Harry Potter and the Sorcerer's Stone

6a. They were just outside / the entrance to the hole, / each one crouching behind a tree / with his gun loaded.

6b. They were just / outside the entrance to the / hole, each one crouching behind a tree with / his gun loaded.

Roald Dahl, Fantastic Mr. Fox

7a. Shrinking is always more / painful than growing, but the / pain was over quickly / enough as I became the size of a cat.

7b. Shrinking is always more painful / than growing, / but the pain was over quickly enough / as I became the size of a cat.

Laurence Yep, Dragon of the Lost Sea

8a. The water snakes moved swiftly, / one after another, / on both sides of the boat, / their pointed heads above water, / making ripples.

8b. The water snakes moved / swiftly, one after / another, on both sides of the boat, their pointed / heads above water, making / ripples.

Jean Craighead George, The Talking Earth

9a. I grabbed Terri's arm as a / shadow swept over us, and an enormous / bat swooped down at / us, red eyes flashing, its pointed / teeth glistening, hissing as it / attacked.

9b. I grabbed Terri's arm / as a shadow swept over us, / and an enormous bat swooped down at us, / red eyes flashing, / its pointed teeth glistening, / hissing as it attacked.

R. L. Stine, Ghost Beach

10a. Trying to look like the / ball players he had seen the time his / father had taken him to the Polo / Ground, Marty ran into the outfield and took the position near the / curb that Gelberg had / selected for him.

10b. Trying to look like the ball players / he had seen / the time his father had taken him to the Polo Ground, / Marty ran into the outfield / and took the position near the curb / that Gelberg had selected for him.

Murray Heyert, "The New Kid"

EXERCISE 2: SPOTTING GOOD CHUNKS

Only five sentences below have good chunks. Spot those five by reading each sentence one slash mark (/) at a time. If it doesn't make sense, that sentence has bad chunks. If it makes sense, you've found a sentence with good chunks.

1. I walked down the / stairs, unbolted the front / door, and stepped out into the morning air.

    Edward Bloor, *Tangerine*

2. The sleet turned to hail, / pelting me / like a swarm of frozen hornets.

    Roland Smith, *Peak*

3. Unlike most / boys his age, he had never begun collecting baseball / cards.

    E. L. Konigsburg, *From the Mixed-Up Files of Mrs. Basil E. Frankweiler*

4. Although it was late in the / afternoon, he was washing the / breakfast dishes.

    Beverly Cleary, *Ramona and Her Father*

5. As he slept, / the dentist saw himself in his speedboat, / flying his airplane, / and living in luxury on the Riviera.

    Chris Van Allsburg, *The Sweetest Fig*

6. At dusk, Sarah cut Caleb's / hair on the front steps, gathering his curls and scattering / them on the / fence and ground.

    Patricia MacLachlan, *Sarah, Plain and Tall*

7. Walking was difficult, because both his / knees were badly / bruised, one ankle / hurting with every step.

    Alexander Key, *The Forgotten Door*

8. When George Washington / took the oath as President, / he had only one tooth left / and continually experimented with different kinds of false teeth / made from ivory, hippo teeth, lead, / and even some of his old teeth recycled.

    Patricia A. Halbert (editor), *I Wish I Knew That: U.S. Presidents*

9. She slung her purse over her shoulder / and walked away, / her stride made uneven by broken sandal thongs, / thin elbows showing through holes / in the oversized sweater, / her jeans faded and baggy.

    Cynthia Voigt, *Homecoming*

10. As much as I would have preferred / to be by myself that first day of school, / I made my way through the lunch line, / picked up my tray of meatloaf, green beans, and Jell-O with banana slices, / then ventured over to a table of boys / that I recognized from some of my classes.

    Clare Vanderpool, *Navigating Early*

EXERCISE 3: MARKING CHUNKS

Copy the sentence, and then divide it with slash marks (/) into good chunks. Remember that each chunk must make sense by itself. **Hint:** Sometimes—but not always—a chunk is punctuated with commas, so look for the commas and you may find the chunks!

1. In the dungeon, there were rats, large rats, mean rats.

    Kate DiCamillo, *The Tale of Despereaux*

2. Between two tall grass blades in the clearing, a spider had spun a web, a circle delicately suspended.

   Ursula K. LeGuin, *Earthsea: The Farthest Shore*

3. He was a rather skinny boy, neither large nor small for fourteen.

   Esther Hoskins Forbes, *Johnny Tremain*

4. She was aware that Johnny was watching her, hoping to find fault, so she swam with deliberate grace.

   Betsy Byars, *The Night Swimmers*

5. The plume of flame suddenly enveloped three of the soldiers, killing them so quickly that they did not even have time to scream.

   Christopher Paolini, *Inheritance*

6. The eagle had two heads, and two necks, coiled around each other like a pair of black feathered snakes, glossy black wings fluttering.

   Scott Westerfeld, *Goliath*

7. Close on me, he stopped and raised on his back legs and hung over me, his forelegs and paws hanging down, weaving back and forth gently as he took his time and decided whether or not to tear my head off.

   Gary Paulsen, *Wood-Song*

8. Dorothy looked at where her house had landed, and, giving a little cry of fright, noticed that just under the corner of the house, the witch's two feet were sticking out, shod in silver shoes with pointed toes.

   L. Frank Baum, *The Wonderful Wizard of Oz*

9. He was Joel bar Hezron, the red-cheeked boy who used to come to
    the synagogue school, the scribe's son, the one the rabbi held up for
    an example, the one they used to tease because his twin sister always
    waited outside to walk home with him.

    Elizabeth George Speare, *The Bronze Bow*

10. Even in the lovely city of Matanzas, with elegant shops and ladies
    in carriages waving silk fans, there was always the scent of rotting
    tropical vegetation, a smell that releases a bit of sorrow, like the death
    of some small wild thing, perhaps a bird or a frog.

    Margarita Engle, *The Firefly Letters*

PARAGRAPH WORKOUT

The paragraph below has chunk marks indicated. Some sentences have just
two chunks, some three, and some more than three. <u>Important</u>: Read out
loud, and pause where each slash mark (/) occurs.

After looking carefully at the author's paragraph and the twin paragraph,
write a triplet paragraph built the same way. Yours should also have three
sentences with the same number of chunks. Build your sentences the way
the sentences are built in the author's paragraph and the twin paragraph.

EXAMPLE

Author's Paragraph

(1) Rachel was an eager skinny little girl / who almost always
wore skirts and blouses / that didn't stay tucked in, / and her nose was
frequently runny / because she had hay fever. (2) Jerry was skinny, too, /
but his nose didn't run. (3) Jerry had black hair, / and Rachel's was
reddish gold, / though / as they sat under the streetlamp, / the hair of
both of them looked purple.

Eleanor Estes, *Ginger Pye*

Twin Paragraph

(1) Peanut was a lovable frisky rescue dog / that always ate dog food and people food / that we mixed together, / and his tail was short / because someone had cut it. (2) Our cat was frisky, too, / but she had a long tail. (3) Peanut had three legs, / and his ears were really weird, / though / when he was lying down, / nothing about his little body seemed strange.

To guide you, here are the sentences side by side from each paragraph.

Author's Paragraph	Twin Paragraph
1. Rachel was an eager skinny little girl / who almost always wore skirts and blouses / that didn't stay tucked in, / and her nose was runny / because she had hay fever.	**1.** Peanut was a lovable frisky rescue dog / that always ate dog food and people food / that we mixed together, / and his tail was short / because someone had cut it.
2. Jerry was skinny, too, / but his nose didn't run.	**2.** Our cat was frisky, too, / but her tail wasn't short.
3. Jerry had black hair, / and Rachel's was reddish gold, / though / as they sat under the streetlamp, / the hair of both of them looked purple.	**3.** Peanut had three legs, / and his ears were really weird, / though / when he was in a deep sleep, / nothing about his little body seemed strange.

REVIEW

Chunks are sentence parts that make sense. Most sentences are made up of chunks that add detail and dazzle to sentences.

PREVIEW

Next you'll imitate great sentences, one chunk (sentence part) at a time, to build your sentences the way authors build theirs.

IMITATING SENTENCES

What are some things you learned to do by watching other people do them—like swinging a bat, making pancakes, buttoning your shirt or blouse, flying a kite, riding a bike? You learned probably by watching people and then imitating what they did.

You can learn how to build strong sentences by imitating authors who know—really, really know—how to build great sentences. They include authors like E. B. White (*Charlotte's Web*), Katherine Paterson (*Bridge to Terabithia*), C. S. Lewis (*The Chronicles of Narnia*), J. R. R. Tolkien (*The Hobbit*), Lemony Snicket (*A Series of Unfortunate Events*), J. K. Rowling (Harry Potter novels), Suzanne Collins (*The Hunger Games*), plus many others whose sentences in this worktext teach you to build sentences like theirs. Those authors are your invisible teachers and your fitness trainers in building better sentences and paragraphs.

Sentence imitating uses an author's model sentence as a blueprint for a twin sentence. You build your twin sentence the same way the author's model sentence is built, but you write about a different topic.

EXAMPLES OF SENTENCE IMITATIONS

Students like you wrote the twin sentences below. Notice how the students built each sentence like the model sentence by the author. After doing the exercises in this section, you, too, will be able to imitate sentences in the same way the students did and receive a gold medal in the sentence-composing Olympics! (Or at least silver or bronze.)

1. *Model:* The cat Chester was curled up on the brown velvet armchair, which years ago he'd staked out as his own.

    Deborah and James Howe, *Bunnicula: A Rabbit-Tale of Mystery*

    Sample Imitation: The girl Samantha was snuggled down under the soft, quilted comforter, which during the night she claimed as her own.

2. *Model:* All day long, the Swan Boats circled the lake, carrying their load of happy people, many of them children.

   > E. B. White, *The Trumpet of the Swan*

   Sample Imitation: All afternoon long, the teenagers played a game, guessing the names of current singers, most of them popular.

3. *Model:* A snowy egret alighted near us and walked gracefully among the reeds, his white plumes falling like lace down his long neck.

   > Jean Craighead George, *The Missing 'Gator of Gumbo Limbo*

   Sample Imitation: Her fat cat jumped upon the sofa and purred contentedly among the pillows, its fuzzy paws moving like hands before its stretched legs.

4. *Model:* The eyes of the black shapes fell on Frodo and pierced him, as they rushed towards him.

   > J. R. R. Tolkien, *The Fellowship of the Ring*

   Sample Imitation: The web of the invisible spider landed on flies and caught them, when they flew into it.

5. *Model:* Slowly the radiance took on form, until it transformed into the body of a great white beast with flowing mane and tail.

   > Madeleine L'Engle, *A Swiftly Tilting Planet*

   Sample Imitation: Gradually the watercolors became a shape, until they created the scene of a quiet gentle street with charming houses and shops.

Imitating sentences is like filling-in a picture in a coloring book. When you color a picture, you're given the shape for the picture, and you add your own colors. When you imitate a sentence, you're given the shape for the sentence, and you add your own words. In the following exercises, you'll learn how.

EXERCISE 1: IDENTIFYING TWIN SENTENCES

To see how they are built alike, copy the model sentence and its twin.

EXAMPLE

Model Sentence: He was in the bushes in moments, scattering the birds, grabbing branches, stripping them to fill his mouth with berries.

Gary Paulsen, *Hatchet*

Sentences

a. The firemen ran up the stairwell, entered the third floor to evacuate the apartments, and directed people to the safest exit.

b. Dad was on the riding mower in the afternoon, cutting the grass, whistling tunes, entertaining himself to pass the time without boredom.

TWIN OF THE MODEL SENTENCE: **b**

Model One: The eagle came back, seized Bilbo in his talons by the back of his coat, and swooped off.

J. R. R. Tolkien, *The Hobbit*

1a. The siren blasted, causing everyone to run out into the street and vacate the premises.

1b. The child walked in, grabbed a donut with the chocolate sprinkles from the tray, and strolled away.

Model Two: Inside the cage there was a tiger, a real, very large tiger, pacing back and forth.

Kate DiCamillo, *The Tiger Rising*

2a. Beside the stream there was a snake, a poisonous, very dangerous snake, slithering in and out.

2b. The large bush occupied a corner of the garden, shielding us from the sun's harsh rays and heat.

Model Three: Sadly, lonesomely, Lucky got into her hot bed, kicking the sheet away.

Susan Patron, *The Higher Power of Lucky*

3a. Quickly, quietly, Brennan took out his new phone, tapping the colorful screen.

3b. Near, far, wherever you looked, seagulls were diving for food along the shore.

Model Four: As I crouched there in the bushes, trying not to fall over the cliff, trying to keep myself hidden and yet to see and hear what went on below me, a boat left the ship.

Scott O'Dell, *Island of the Blue Dolphins*

4a. While I waited then at the scene, trying not to make a loud noise, attempting to listen very carefully and so to notice and record what went on around me, a policeman entered the area.

4b. As I thought about all the games that had happened during the summer, during the winning streaks of June and July and August, I became excited to enter the finals for the championship.

Model Five: Harry twisted his body around and saw a grindylow, a small, horned water demon, poking out of the weed, its long fingers clutched tightly around Harry's leg, its pointed fangs bared.

J. K. Rowling, *Harry Potter and the Goblet of Fire*

5a. Mrs. Cranston had trouble understanding why the room needed to be redecorated because it was a lovely, small, inviting room that everyone found charming, with windows with lace curtains.

5b. Nina looked out the window and saw a tornado, a dark, menacing black twister, crossing over the field, its high funnel zigzagging across the land, its dangerous path unpredictable.

EXERCISE 2: FINDING TWIN SENTENCES

Match the twin sentence with its model sentence.

Model Sentences	Twin Sentences
1. A thousand live bats fluttered from the walls and ceiling while a thousand more swooped over the tables in low black clouds. J. K. Rowling, *Harry Potter and the Sorcerer's Stone*	**a.** Talking is often more interesting than listening, but his talk was never interesting enough so my mind wandered from the topic.
2. They were just outside the entrance to the hole, each one crouching behind a tree with his gun loaded. Roald Dahl, *Fantastic Mr. Fox*	**b.** The amazing chipmunks darted quickly, one after another, in every part of the yard, their bodies racing, creating blurs.
3. Shrinking is always more painful than growing, but the pain was over quickly enough as I became the size of a cat. Laurence Yep, *Dragon of the Lost Sea*	**c.** They were now inside the entrance of the castle, every one looking toward the gloom with their hearts racing.
4. The water snakes moved swiftly, one after another, on both sides of the boat, their pointed heads above water, making ripples. Jean Craighead George, *The Talking Earth*	**d.** Kylie protected Nicole's eyes as the dust came toward us, and an insect cloud surrounded us, black specks swarming, their sound deafening, buzzing as they landed.

5. I grabbed Terri's arm as a shadow swept over us, and an enormous bat swooped down at us, red eyes flashing, its pointed teeth glistening, hissing as it attacked. R. L. Stine, *Ghost Beach*	**e.** A hundred lovely flowers bloomed in the meadow and road, while a hundred more filled up the house in vibrant varied colors.

EXERCISE 3: UNSCRAMBLING IMITATIONS

Unscramble and write out the sentence parts to imitate the model sentence. Then write your own sentence imitation with sentence parts like the model. Tell about something from a TV show, movie, story—or your imagination.

EXAMPLE

Model Sentence: I unhooked the wire, pushed the fence open, and led Shiloh to the stream for a drink, filling the pie pan with fresh water.

Phyllis Reynolds Naylor, *Shiloh*

Scrambled Sentence Parts

a. opened the closet door

b. beside the scarf

c. I removed my coat

d. and placed the coat in the back

e. hanging my favorite coat with gentle care

Unscrambled Imitation: I removed my coat, opened the closet door, and placed the coat in the back beside the scarf, hanging my favorite coat with gentle care.

Sample Student Imitation: Skylar took a bath, washed her long hair, and cleaned the tub with the cleanser from the shelf, scrubbing its white surface with strong strokes.

----

1. Didi went to the stove, finished cooking the eggs, put them on a plate, and ate them.

   Walter Dean Myers, *Motown and Didi*

   1a. checked the list of reservations

   1b. and seated them

   1c. the hostess went to the podium

   1d. escorted the guests into the dining room

2. Without warning, two yellow eyes surfaced just above the water line.

   Patricia C. McKissack, *A Million Fish . . . More or Less*

   2a. into the clear pool

   2b. dove together

   2c. in sync

   2d. two Olympic divers

3. A tuna fish, swift, fierce, and very hungry, came darting through the waves.

   Leo Lionni, *Swimmy*

   3a. sat crying on the bench

   3b. and very frightened

   3c. the lost girl

   3d. tiny, alone

4. When I was certain both of them were soundly asleep, I fetched Mandy's other present, the book of fairy tales, out of my bag.

    Gail Carson Levine, *Ella Enchanted*

    4a. inside of his security box

    4b. after I verified that both of the documents were absolutely authentic

    4c. the list of soldiers' names

    4d. I examined Harold's final document

5. Ferdinand didn't look where he was sitting, and instead of sitting on the nice, cool grass in the shade, he sat on a bumble bee.

    Munro Leaf, *The Story of Ferdinand*

    5a. she missed all the directions

    5b. Josie didn't hear

    5c. and instead of listening to the calm, clear instructions of her teacher

    5d. what he was saying

EXERCISE 4: WRITING IMITATIONS

PART ONE

Look closely at the model and a sample imitation, and then write your own imitation.

1. *Model:* In the fishpond, the hippo belched, not softly.

    Leon Hugo, "My Father and the Hippopotamus"

    Student Imitation: At the bus stop, Christine smiled, not shyly.

2. ***Model:*** Suddenly, a few large drops of rain splattered into the dust.

    Carolyn Keene, *The Secret of Shadow Ranch*

    Student Imitation: Painlessly, the tiny piece of skin detached from the finger.

3. ***Model:*** Down fell the snow on top of Peter's head.

    Ezra Jack Keats, *The Snowy Day*

    Student Imitation: Up jumped the crowd from their seats in the bleachers.

4. ***Model:*** They unwrapped the blanket, and there in the center was a tiny black and white rabbit, sitting in a shoebox filled with dirt.

    Deborah and James Howe, *Bunnicula: A Rabbit-Tale of Mystery*

    Student Imitation: The detective opened the closet, and there in the back was an antique gray and blue box, lying in the corner full of shoes.

5. ***Model:*** It was a runt, a piglet born for some reason far smaller and weaker than its brothers and sisters.

    Dick King-Smith, *Pigs Might Fly*

    Student Imitation: It was a surprise, a package wrapped for her birthday, much prettier and bigger than her other presents.

PART TWO

Copy the model sentence and the one sentence that imitates it. Then imitate the same model sentence, telling about something from a TV show, movie, story—or your imagination. When you finish, you will have three sentences built the same way—the model sentence, the sample imitation sentence, and your own imitation sentence.

6. *Model:* In the very heart of the fire, underneath the kettle, was a huge, black egg.

> J. K. Rowling, *Harry Potter and the Sorcerer's Stone*

   a. After the excitement of the championship game, they gathered to get everyone together to celebrate.

   b. Across the field from the barn, near a herd of cattle, were several groups of contestants.

   c. Near the farthest corner of the attic, beside the trunk, was a broken, antique bowl.

7. *Model:* Unearthly humps of land curved into the darkening sky like the backs of pigs, like the rumps of elephants.

> Enid Bagnold, *National Velvet*

   a. Beautiful clouds in the blue sky suggested clear weather, a beautiful night, with clear sky and full moon.

   b. Disorganized piles of paper scattered over the office desk like some confetti from parades, like shredded records of accountants.

   c. Swarms of insects crossed over the meadow, searching for water during the drought during the scorching heat wave.

8. *Model:* If you are interested in stories with happy endings, you would be better off reading some other book.

> Lemony Snicket, *The Bad Beginning*

   a. You are not always, when you are hoping for a wonderful present, going to be pleased.

   b. When you are searching for people with interesting lives, you would be richly rewarded reading certain biographies.

   c. After eating the delicious meal, they were overjoyed when the server brought a surprise birthday cake.

9. *Model:* At the top of the bank, close to the wild cherry where the blackbird sang, was a little group of holes almost hidden by brambles.

Richard Adams, Watership Down

   a. Near the bottom of the stream, up above some colored stones where the water slowed, was a camouflaged school of guppies safely protected from predators.

   b. In the late afternoon, when the dazzling sun was about to set on the horizon, there were watercolored markings throughout the meadow.

   c. In the field of wild flowers and grass, where often rabbits came to nibble, my teacher used to take us to study nature.

10. *Model:* Once, when she had to dip about a thousand chicken pieces into some disgusting yellow stuff and lay them in deep friers, she had to run out and throw up.

Lynne Reid Banks, One More River

   a. Once, while a storm raged through the neighborhood, she had tried to keep her brothers and sister from being terrified, diverting them with stories.

   b. Probably, there was no reason for them to be suspicious of the small group of travelers lining up by the side of the road near the depot.

   c. Always, when he had to run about a million long laps during the sweltering summer heat and keep pace around the track, he had to reach down and find grit.

PARAGRAPH WORKOUT

Write a paragraph (<u>five to ten sentences</u>) to create an incident that could appear in any Harry Potter story (or some other story you like).

Within your paragraph, include imitations of *three* of the model sentences below by J. K. Rowling, author of the Harry Potter stories. Build all of your sentences—*not just the three imitations*—the way authors build their sentences.

MODEL SENTENCES BY J. K. ROWLING

From *Harry Potter and the Sorcerer's Stone*

Slowly, very slowly, the snake raised its head until its eyes were on a level with Harry's.

From *Harry Potter and the Chamber of Secrets*

The room was dingy and windowless, lit by a single oil lamp dangling from the low ceiling.

From *Harry Potter and the Prisoner of Azkaban*

A voice came suddenly out of the shadows, a soft, misty sort of voice.

From *Harry Potter and the Goblet of Fire*

Bloodthirsty and brutal, the giants brought themselves to the point of extinction by warring amongst themselves during the last century.

From *Harry Potter and the Order of the Phoenix*

Standing still and quiet in the gloom, the creatures looked eerie and sinister.

From *Harry Potter and the Half-Blood Prince*

Stupefied, painted gold, stuffed into a miniature tutu and with small wings glued to its back, it glowered down at them all, the ugliest angel Harry had ever seen, with a large bald head like a potato and rather hairy feet.

From *Harry Potter and the Deathly Hallows*

He was also sure that ghouls were generally rather slimy and bald, rather than distinctly hairy and covered in angry purple blisters.

- Exchange your draft with other students for suggestions to improve your paragraph, and also give them suggestions for improving theirs.

- Then revise several times until your paragraph is finished.

- Give your paragraph a catchy title.

REVIEW

Imitating sentences by authors is like filling in colors within the lines of a coloring book. An author gives you the shape of the sentence, and you fill it in with your own words.

PREVIEW

Unscrambling sentences of authors is like a jigsaw puzzle. You get mixed-up parts and have to arrange them into a good sentence, sort of like puzzle pieces arranged to make a good picture.

UNSCRAMBLING SENTENCES

Unless they're eggs, things scrambled—like clothes in a drawer or closet, toys scattered around on the floor, stuff strewn across the basement or attic—are a jumbled mess. They drive people crazy because people want order in their lives, not jumbled messes. Getting order and neatness takes work, though. You probably remember times you were told to straighten your room, and, looking around at the stuff strewn all over, didn't know where to start.

Getting order and neatness in sentences and paragraphs also takes work. Readers want your sentences and paragraphs to be orderly and neat, with your paragraph's sentence parts and sentences in proper places, not in jumbled messes.

EXAMPLE

The sentence describes a polar bear eating a seal.

Scrambled Sentence Parts
a. turning back the skin and blubber

b. and ate greedily of the hot crimson meat

c. the polar bear ripped up the seal's body

d. letting out a cloud of steam

Unscrambled Sentences (Two make sense. One doesn't make sense.)

1. The polar bear ripped up the seal's body, turning back the skin and blubber, letting out a cloud of steam, and ate greedily of the hot crimson meat.

2. And ate greedily of the hot crimson meat, turning back the skin and blubber, the polar bear ripped up the seal's body, letting out a cloud of steam.

3. The polar bear ripped up the seal's body, letting out a cloud of steam, turning back the skin and blubber, and ate greedily of the hot crimson meat.

The first version is the one Norah Burke wrote in "Polar Night." The third version is also unscrambled well. The second version, though, doesn't make much sense because the bear cannot eat the meat of the seal before removing the skin that covers the seal's flesh.

EXERCISE 1: UNSCRAMBLING SENTENCE PARTS

Unscramble each sentence twice. One should make sense, but the other shouldn't make sense. Tell why that one doesn't make sense.

Note: Use commas for pauses.

1a. twice a year

1b. she had her eye on Henry Piper

1c. who came to town

1d. the young farm machinery salesman

> Bill Brittain, *The Wish Giver*

2a. on her upper lip

2b. when they set down their empty soda glasses

2c. had a chocolate moustache

2d. each of the ladies

> Ray Bradbury, "The Whole Town's Sleeping"

3a. was a skunk

3b. and there

3c. he looked behind him

3d. coming out of the woods

E. B. White, The Trumpet of the Swan

4a. popped her into his waistcoat pocket

4b. the Big Friendly Giant

4c. and

4d. before Sophie could protest

4e. picked her up off the table

Roald Dahl, The BFG

5a. like the snow

5b. and they can sneak up

5c. so that they will be harder to see

5d. on their next meal

5e. polar bears are white

Susan Patron, The Higher Power of Lucky

6a. like the burrows the real rabbits lived in

6b. sleeping in the boy's bed

6c. for the Boy made nice tunnels for him

6d. the velveteen rabbit grew to like

6e. under the bedclothes that he said were

Margery Williams, The Velveteen Rabbit

7a. curled herself up

7b. opened a book

7c. Sara

7d. and began to read

7e. in the window-seat

Frances Hodgson Burnett, *A Little Princess*

8a. a hollow that had been cleared of trees

8b. craning his neck sideways

8c. so that the stars shone brightly

8d. he realized that they had reached the ridge of a vast hollow

8e. onto the worst scene he had ever laid eyes on

J. K. Rowling, *Harry Potter and the Chamber of Secrets*

9a. watched the cat

9b. curl himself

9c. he

9d. on the lap

9e. well-fed and content

9f. of one of the sleepy children by the fire

Sheila Burnford, *The Incredible Journey*

10a. and every night

10b. she watched her

10c. pull down her ragged torn web

10d. every morning

10e. weave a new one

10f. Maggie watched the spider

Jean Craighead George, *The Fire Bug Connection*

EXERCISE 2: PLACING SENTENCE PARTS

Move the underlined sentence parts to another place that makes sense.

EXAMPLE

Original Arrangement

<u>In a surprisingly short time</u>, he grew to recognize individual fish and to know where to find them.

New Arrangement

He grew to recognize individual fish <u>in a surprisingly short time</u> and to know where to find them.

---

1. <u>Uneasily</u>, Beezus sat down in the living room to try to think while she listened to the silence.

Beverly Cleary, *Beezus and Ramona*

2. Rainsford sprang up and moved quickly to the rail, <u>mystified</u>.

Richard Connell, "The Most Dangerous Game"

3. <u>Down, down</u> she went, faster and faster, into the forest below.

Janell Cannon, *Stellaluna*

4. <u>When they heard the fire engine</u>, the children in the school across the street couldn't keep their eyes on their lessons.

Virginia Lee Burton, *Mike Mulligan and His Steam Shovel*

5. If you look cute, you are cute, and if you look smart, you are smart.

    Betsy Byars, *The Summer of the Swans*

6. That afternoon, a big man came and pried off the drain cover, grunting as he worked.

    Pam Conrad, "The Tub People"

7. Staring at the glowing bright green eyes of the tyrannosaur, he could feel his knees begin to shake uncontrollably, his trousers flapping like flags.

    Michael Crichton, *Jurassic Park*

8. Deep in the pine woods, along a deserted logging road, the boy and dog came to a small open space where there had once been a log ramp.

    William H. Armstrong, *Sounder*

9. One morning, smiling prettily, and swinging her lunch box, Ramona skipped to school.

    Beverly Cleary, *Ramona and Her Father*

10. In the evenings, after he had finished his supper of watery cabbage soup, Charlie always went into the room of his four grandparents to listen to their stories.

    Roald Dahl, *Charlie and the Chocolate Factory*

PARAGRAPH WORKOUT

You learned that there is more than one way to arrange sentence parts within a sentence. All arrangements are fine—unless they are scrambled messes.

Now you have to straighten out a big, scrambled mess. Sentence parts have been removed from the following paragraph and then scrambled. Underneath the stripped-down version of the paragraph is the scrambled list of sentence parts.

Directions: Insert the scrambled sentence parts where they belong into the stripped-down paragraph.

STRIPPED-DOWN PARAGRAPH

(1) Matilda's speech was perfect, and she knew as many words as most grown-ups. (2) Her parents called her a noisy chatterbox and told her that little girls should be seen and not heard. (3) Matilda had taught herself to read. (4) She could read fast and well, and she naturally began hankering after books. (5) The only book in this enlightened household was something called *Easy Cooking*. (6) She decided she wanted something more interesting.

from *Matilda* by Roald Dahl

a. belonging to Matilda's mother

b. at the age of four

c. when she had read this from cover to cover and had learned all the recipes by heart

d. by studying newspapers and magazines that lay around the house

e. instead of applauding her

f. by the age of one and a half

g. by the time she was three

REVIEW

Putting things in the right places is important, whether it's in your room, or in your sentences. If your room is a jumbled mess, you can't find things. If your sentence is a jumbled mess, your readers can't find meaning.

PREVIEW

Using a variety of sentence-composing tools within your paragraphs is also important. Nobody likes boredom. Variety is the solution.

VARYING PARAGRAPHS

We all like variety in what we do, in what we eat, in what we play, in what we read, and in just about everything else. Good writers know the need to provide variety for their readers, including sentence variety in their paragraphs.

You may have heard that "variety is the spice of life." In the following exercises, you'll practice ways to add spice to paragraphs through variety in sentence-composing tools.

EXERCISE 1: PLACING TOOLS

In the paragraphs below, practice tool variety by moving each underlined sentence part to another good place within the same sentence. Write out the new paragraphs.

PARAGRAPH ONE (from *Harry Potter and the Chamber of Secrets* by J. K. Rowling)

(1) On the other side of the dungeon was a long table, <u>covered in black velvet</u>. (2) They approached it eagerly but next moment had stopped in their tracks, <u>horrified</u>. (3) The smell was quite disgusting. (4) Large, rotten fish were laid on handsome silver platters. (5) Cakes, <u>burned charcoal-black</u>, were heaped on salvers. (6) There was a great maggoty haggis, a slab of cheese covered in furry green mold and, <u>in pride of place</u>, an enormous gray cake in the shape of a tombstone, <u>with tar-like icing</u>. (7) Harry watched, <u>amazed</u>, as a portly ghost approached the table, crouched low, and walked through it, <u>his mouth held wide so that it passed through one of the stinking salmon</u>.

PARAGRAPH TWO (from *The Hobbit* by J. R. R. Tolkien)

(1) Gollum wanted that ring <u>because it was a ring of power</u>. (2) Gollum used to wear it <u>at first</u>, till it tired him. (3) <u>Then</u> he kept it in a pouch next his skin, till it galled him. (4) <u>Now</u> usually he hid it in a

hole in the rock on his island, and was always going back to look at it. (5) Still sometimes he put it on, <u>when he could not bear to be parted from it any longer</u>, or when he was very, very, hungry, and tired of eating fish. (6) Then he would creep along dark passages, <u>looking for stray goblins</u>. (7) No one would see him or notice him, <u>till he had his fingers on their throat</u>.

PARAGRAPH THREE (from *Leviathan* by Scott Westerfeld)

(1) Alek turned and peered at the gap beneath his bed chamber's double doors. (2) Shadows shifted along the sliver of moonlight, and he heard the hiss of whispers. (3) Someone was right outside. (4) <u>Silent in bare feet</u>, he swiftly crossed the cold marble floor, sliding into bed just as the door creaked open. (5) Alex narrowed his eyes to a slit, <u>wondering which of the servants was checking on him</u>. (6) Moonlight spilled into the room, <u>making the tin soldiers on his desk glitter</u>. (7) Someone slipped inside, <u>graceful and dead silent</u>. (8) The figure paused, <u>staring at Alex for a moment</u>, then crept toward his dresser. (9) Alex heard the wooden rasp of a drawer sliding open. (10) His heart raced.

EXERCISE 2: PLACING AND CREATING TOOLS

In the paragraphs, put each underlined tool in a new effective place within the same sentence. Also, for each caret (^), create a tool to insert.

EXAMPLE

(1) <u>Beyond the noise of his own sobs</u>, Matt heard a voice calling, ^ . (2) Matt ran to the window, ^ . (3) Then a shadow crossed the opening, and Matt recoiled so quickly that he fell over, ^ . (4) The door handle rattled as Matt squatted on the floor, <u>his heart pounding</u>. (5) Someone, <u>cupping his hands to see through the gloom</u>, put his face against the window.

from *The House of the Scorpion* by Nancy Farmer

Note: Repositioned tools are <u>underlined</u>. Created tools are **bolded**.

(1) Matt heard, <u>beyond the noise of his own sobs,</u> a voice calling, **a child's voice.** (2) Matt ran to the window, **where he saw nothing unusual.** (3) Then a shadow crossed the opening, and Matt recoiled so quickly that he fell over, **landing on the floor.** (4) The door handle rattled as Matt, <u>his heart pounding,</u> squatted on the floor. (5) Someone put his face against the window, <u>cupping his hands to see through the gloom.</u>

PARAGRAPH ONE (from *A Man in Full* by Tom Wolfe)

(1) The snake's huge mouth, ^ , was wide open. (2) Its two fangs, <u>truly like hypodermic needles,</u> were erect. (3) It bit at the air, and great gouts of yellowish venom spurted from the fangs, ^ . (4) Its forked black tongue flicked in every direction, <u>a hissing sound bursting from its throat.</u>

PARAGRAPH TWO (from *Harry Potter and the Prisoner of Azkaban* by J. K. Rowling)

(1) Harry, <u>though still rather small and skinny for his age,</u> had grown a few inches over the last year. (2) His jet-black hair, however, was just as it always had been, <u>stubbornly untidy, whatever he did to it.</u> (3) ^, the eyes behind his glasses, ^, were bright green. (4) On his forehead, clearly visible through his hair, was a thin scar, <u>shaped like a bolt of lightning.</u>

PARAGRAPH THREE (from *Tangerine* by Edward Bloor)

(1) I woke up in the dark to the sound of an explosion, ^ . (2) I groped around for my regular glasses, <u>unable to find them in this new</u>

bedroom, upstairs in this new house. (3) Then my glasses suddenly appeared on the nightstand, illumined by a flash of light. (4) I'd no sooner pulled them on when another explosion, ^ , made the windows rattle and the walls shake. (5) The lightning once again filled the room, painful and surprising, like the flash of a camera in my face. (6) ^ , I waited for more explosions to follow, but none did, and, ^ , I fell back asleep.

SENTENCE-COMPOSING TOOLS

Look at the two paragraphs below to see the huge difference those tools make, kind of like adding pepperoni (or sausage or peppers or hamburg or onions or olives or shrimp or some combination to a pizza).

The paragraph describes the terrifying near-death of Holly, a super-intelligent fairy, inside a burning pod hurled by an enemy through space to what could be her death.

PARAGRAPH WITHOUT TOOLS

(1) The burning flare caught Holly like a hurricane. (2) Rocks pelted the craft's underside. (3) The heat was enough to fry a human. (4) The acceleration dragged at her body with invisible hands. (5) Holly blinked salty sweat from her eyes. (6) The burning flare had totally engulfed her pod. (7) Orange-striped magma swirled around her. (8) The pod groaned and complained. (9) She felt like a nut inside a shell. (10) A bow plate buckled. (11) Her eyes would be first to go. (12) Holly sealed the helmet to protect her eyes. (82 WORDS)

PARAGRAPH WITH SENTENCE-COMPOSING TOOLS

(1) The burning flare caught Holly like a hurricane, spinning the pod at first until the fins caught. (2) Rocks, half-melted, pelted the craft's underside, jolting it toward the chute walls. (3) The heat,

tremendous in the confined space, was enough to fry a human, <u>but fairy lungs like Holly's are made of stronger stuff</u>. (4) The acceleration dragged at her body with invisible hands, <u>stretching the flesh over her arms and face</u>. (5) Holly blinked salty sweat from her eyes, <u>concentrating on the monitor</u>. (6) The burning flare had totally engulfed her pod, <u>a big one, too, force seven at the very least, a good thousand-foot girth</u>. (7) Orange-striped magma swirled around her, <u>hissing, searching for a weak point in the metal casing</u>. (8) The pod groaned and complained, <u>fifty-year-old rivets threatening to pop</u>. (9) She felt like a nut inside a shell, <u>between a gnome's molars, doomed</u>. (10) A bow plate buckled, <u>popped in as though punched by a giant fist, with Holly's head being squeezed</u>. (11) Her eyes would be first to go, <u>popping like ripe berries</u>. (12) Holly sealed the helmet to protect her eyes, <u>riding out the final barrage of rocks</u>. (184 WORDS)

Eoin Colfer, Artemis Fowl (adapted)

Look at the paragraphs' sentences side by side to see how sentence-composing tools add detail and dazzle to the paragraph.

1a. The burning flare caught Holly like a hurricane.

1b. The burning flare caught Holly like a hurricane, <u>spinning the pod at first until the fins caught</u>.

2a. Rocks pelted the craft's underside.

2b. Rocks, <u>half-melted</u>, pelted the craft's underside, <u>jolting it toward the chute walls</u>.

3a. The heat was enough to fry a human.

3b. The heat, <u>tremendous in the confined space</u>, was enough to fry a human, <u>but fairy lungs like Holly's are made of stronger stuff</u>.

4a. The acceleration dragged at her body with invisible hands.

4b. The acceleration dragged at her body with invisible hands, <u>stretching the flesh over her arms and face</u>.

5a. Holly blinked salty sweat from her eyes.

5b. Holly blinked salty sweat from her eyes, <u>concentrating on the monitor</u>.

6a. The burning flare had totally engulfed her pod.

6b. The burning flare had totally engulfed her pod, <u>a big one, too, force seven at the very least, a good thousand-foot girth</u>.

7a. Orange-striped magma swirled around her.

7b. Orange-striped magma swirled around her, <u>hissing, searching for a weak point in the metal casing</u>.

8a. The pod groaned and complained.

8b. The pod groaned and complained, <u>fifty-year-old rivets threatening to pop</u>.

9a. She felt like a nut inside a shell.

9b. She felt like a nut inside a shell, <u>between a gnome's molars, doomed</u>.

10a. A bow plate buckled.

10b. A bow plate buckled, <u>popped in as though punched by a giant fist, with Holly's head being squeezed</u>.

11a. Her eyes would be first to go.

11b. Her eyes would be first to go, <u>popping like ripe berries</u>.

12a. Holly sealed the helmet to protect her eyes.

12b. Holly sealed the helmet to protect her eyes, <u>riding out the final barrage of rocks</u>.

In a paragraph, power comes from details. Details come from the kind of sentence-composing tools underlined above. You can learn, own, and use the same tools to build your sentences for elaboration in your paragraphs. Now give it a try.

PARAGRAPH WORKOUT

The next paragraphs are stripped-down versions with tools removed. Without those tools, they lose power. To restore tool power, create for each sentence at least one tool and place it effectively. Use a variety of tool places: beginning of the sentence, middle of the sentence, or end of the sentence. Also, use a variety of tool lengths: short, medium, long.

PARAGRAPH ONE (from *The Hunger Games* by Suzanne Collins)

(1) There are my wounds to contend with. (2) I treat my burns with the ointment and try dabbing a bit on my stings as well, but it has no effect on them. (3) My mother knew a treatment for them, but she seldom had cause to use it, and I don't even remember its name let alone its appearance.

PARAGRAPH TWO (from *Prince Caspian* by C. S. Lewis)

(1) The luggage, the seat, the platform, and the train station had completely vanished. (2) The four children found themselves standing in a woody place, and there was hardly room to move. (3) They all took a deep breath. (4) They were back in Narnia.

PARAGRAPH THREE (from *The Witches* by Roald Dahl)

(1) My grandmother enthralled me with every story she told me. (2) She was tremendously old and wrinkled. (3) Grandmother sat there majestic in her armchair. (4) Not even a mouse could have squeezed in to sit beside her. (5) I myself was crouched on the floor by her feet.

REVIEW

Sentence-composing tools build better sentences and paragraphs by adding detail and dazzle.

PREVIEW

You learned earlier how to imitate authors' sentences. Paragraphs are made up of sentences, so now you'll be able to imitate their paragraphs, too, one sentence at a time.

IMITATING PARAGRAPHS

You can easily spot twins, not just twin people, but look-alikes of any kind: cars, houses, hairstyles, clothes, shoes—just about anything twin. You learned about twin sentences earlier. In this section you'll practice spotting twin paragraphs because both paragraphs are built alike.

EXERCISE 1: SPOTTING THE TWIN PARAGRAPH

Read the model paragraph and the two paragraphs underneath it. Which *one* of the two paragraphs is the model paragraph's twin because it imitates the way the sentences in the model paragraph are built?

MODEL PARAGRAPH ONE

(1) There are two good reasons to put your napkin in your lap. (2) One is that food might spill in your lap, and it is better to stain the napkin than your clothing. (3) The other is that it can serve as a perfect hiding place. (4) Practically nobody is nosy enough to take the napkin off a lap to see what is hidden there. (5) I sighed deeply and stared down at my lap, as if I were lost in thought, and then, quickly and quietly, I unfolded and read the note the woman had dropped there.

Lemony Snicket, *Who Could That Be at This Hour?*

Paragraph A

(1) Here are two good reasons to put shoes on your feet. (2) One is that mud might land around your toes, and it is better to muddy the shoes than your toes. (3) The other is that they can act as a powerful fashion statement. (4) Almost everyone is interested enough to choose the shoes for their feet to demonstrate what is stylish then. (5) I walked slowly and looked down at my feet, because I was looking for problems, and then, suddenly and luckily, I found and avoided the rocks the storm had left underneath.

Paragraph B

(1) People wear shoes for mainly two good reasons. (2) If you don't wear shoes, and just go barefoot outside in rain, you could get muddy toes, but with shoes on, you won't get your feet all muddy. (3) Some people use shoes to show they are very aware of new shoe fashions. (4) Those people take a lot of time when selecting shoes that make a fashion statement. (5) One day, I was out walking and looked at my shoes, but was lucky enough to avoid stepping on rocks left by a recent storm.

MODEL PARAGRAPH TWO

(1) The body is marvelous at letting us know how much water we need. (2) Diet, exercise, and the environment all play a role. (3) If you eat lots of foods naturally rich in water, such as vegetables, fruits, and whole grains, you may not need to drink much water. (4) If you don't eat salty foods, you need less drinking water. (5) Doctors say that the best guide to how much water we need is our sense of thirst.

Larry Scheckel, *Ask Your Science Teacher*

Paragraph A

(1) People can control their thoughts, and can think just about anything. (2) Our thoughts are made up of our experiences. (3) The best way is to think happy thoughts so that you don't have to deal with lots of unpleasant thoughts. (4) People who think mainly pleasant thoughts don't want to control their thoughts because they enjoy those thoughts and don't want to change them. (5) People who study how people think agree that optimistic thoughts are best.

Paragraph B

(1) The mind is amazing at helping us think whatever we wish. (2) People, places, and situations all contribute to thought. (3) If you

think lots of thoughts very optimistic in content, such as memories, projections, and pleasant wishes, you may not need to control your thoughts. (4) If you don't think horrible thoughts, you need less thought control. (5) Psychologists say that the best guide to how much optimism we feel is our control of thoughts.

MODEL PARAGRAPH THREE

(1) Harry missed Hogwarts School of Witchcraft and Wizardry so much it was like having a constant stomachache. (2) He missed the castle with its secret passageways and ghosts, his classes, the mail arriving by owl, eating banquets in the Great Hall, sleeping in his four-poster bed in the tower dormitory, visiting Hagrid, the game-keeper, in his cabin in the Forbidden Forest. (3) Especially he missed Quidditch, the most popular sport in the wizarding world.

J. K. Rowling, *Harry Potter and the Chamber of Secrets*

Paragraph A

(1) Loving Cape May, New Jersey so much, Jenny felt it was like having a warm glow. (2) She loved the white sand and sandpipers on the beach, the way the sunsets spilled over the ocean, breakfast on the boardwalk, the tiny apartment a block from the beach in which they stayed, and about one block from the beach their visits to their old house called Jefferson Place. (3) She especially loved the most energizing event in that seaside town, surfing.

Paragraph B

(1) Jenny loved Cape May, New Jersey so much it was like having a warm glow. (2) She loved the beach with its white sand and sandpipers, the sun, the sunsets spilling over the ocean, having breakfast on the boardwalk, staying in their tiny apartment a block from the beach, visiting Jefferson Place, their old house, about one block from the

beach. (3) Especially she loved surfing, the most energizing event in that seaside town.

MODEL PARAGRAPH FOUR

(1) At the far end of the attic there was a small window, and along the wall beside it were some cardboard boxes. (2) In them were the things that Elizabeth had stored when she put the house up for rent after her mother's death. (3) Seating herself on the wooden support next to the first of the boxes, Nancy stretched her legs out for balance and began to investigate the contents. (4) This box contained clothing, dresses, and gloves and shoes, an assortment of odd, old-fashioned hats, and a christening gown for a baby. (5) The gown was yellow with age, so Nancy lifted it out carefully.

Lois Duncan, *A Gift of Magic*

Paragraph A

(1) Some storage bins were located next to a locked door in the back of the activity room. (2) When Sanford became chairman of the athletic department after his predecessor's retirement, Sanford had moved those bins that contained athletic equipment. (3) After George put himself on the gymnastic mat, George settled his body on the gymnastic mat next to the first of the bins to start inventorying the items. (4) Rackets, balls, and this and that were in one of the bins, plus a collection of old outdated uniforms and a faded gymnast's leotard. (5) Covered with dust, the leotard was slowly shaken by George.

Paragraph B

(1) In the back of the activity room there was a locked door, and in the space beside it were some storage bins. (2) In them was the athletic equipment that Sanford had moved when he became the chairman of the athletic department after his predecessor's retirement. (3) Putting

himself on the gymnastic mat next to the first of the bins, George settled his body on the mat and started to inventory the items. (4) One bin had rackets, balls, and this and that, a collection of old outdated uniforms and a faded leotard for a gymnast. (5) The leotard was covered with dust, so George shook it out slowly.

MODEL PARAGRAPH FIVE

(1) Sullivan ambled down a stretch of land, crossed the street, and sat down on the wooden sidewalk. (2) Adjusting his wooden leg to make himself comfortable, he leaned back against the fence to enjoy the night. (3) The wind, coming off the prairie, had been strong all day, gusting wildly sometimes, with leaves scuttling across the street. (4) While he pushed himself up to go home, he first saw the fire, a single tongue of flame shooting out the side of O'Leary's barn. (5) Sullivan made his way directly to the barn to save the animals inside. (6) The barn's loft held over three tons of hay, delivered earlier that day. (7) Flames from the burning hay pushed against the roof and beams, as if they were struggling to break free. (8) A shower of burning embers greeted Sullivan as he entered the building. (9) The heat was fiercely intense and blinding. (10) In his rush to flee, Sullivan slipped on the uneven floorboards and fell with a thud. (11) As he struggled to get up, Sullivan discovered that his wooden leg had gotten stuck between two boards and come off.

Jim Murphy, *The Great Fire*

Paragraph A

(1) Ingmar walked across a stretch of beach, approached a rock, and sat down on its cold surface. (2) Spreading his blanket to make the rock warmer, he settled down on his perch to watch the ocean. (3) The sun, reflecting off the sea, had been muted all day, sometimes disappearing

completely, with clouds covering over the warmth. (4) While he packed up his blanket to leave the beach, Ingmar first saw the boat, a battered piece of sail falling over the side of a small skiff. (5) Ingmar made his way quickly to the shore to signal the people onboard. (6) The small skiff held a group of tourists, frightened by their plight. (7) Waves from the cold ocean washed over the skiff and passengers, as if the waves were planning to capsize all. (8) A chorus of shrill voices hit Ingmar as he waved his arms. (9) The water was very cold and churning. (10) In his hurry to help, Ingmar jumped into the icy surf and yelled with encouragement. (11) Although he wanted to swim out, Ingmar realized that his seaside outing had resulted in high drama and turned dark.

Paragraph B

(1) Walking across a stretch of beach, Ingmar approached a rock, and sat down on its cold surface. (2) He spread his blanket to make the rock warmer, and then he settled down on his perch to watch the ocean. (3) All day the sun, reflecting off the sea, had been muted, and sometimes it disappeared completely, and the clouds covered over the warmth. (4) Ingmar first saw the boat while packing up his blanket to leave the beach, and he saw a battered piece of sail falling over the side of a small skiff. (5) Quickly, to signal the people onboard, Ingmar made his way to the shore. (6) A group of tourists, who were frightened by their plight, was in the small skiff. (7) It seemed as if the cold waves, washing over the skiff and passengers, were planning to capsize all. (8) As Ingmar waved his arms, a chorus of shrill voices hit Ingmar. (9) The very cold water was churning. (10) Ingmar, in his hurry to help, yelling with encouragement, jumped into the icy surf. (11) Ingmar, although he wanted to swim out, realized that his seaside outing, resulting in high drama, had turned dark.

SUMMARY

Paragraph imitating uses an author's model paragraph as a blueprint for a twin paragraph. A twin paragraph has sentences built like those in the author's paragraph, but is written about a different topic.

EXAMPLE

Model Paragraph

(1) There are several kinds of silence. (2) There's the silence of being alone, which I like well enough. (3) Then there's the silence of one's father when you have nothing to say, and he has nothing to say. (4) There's the silence between you after the investigation of your stepmother's death.

Fanny Billingsley, *Chime*

Twin Paragraph

(1) There are several kinds of laughter. (2) There's the laughter of spontaneous humor, which I always enjoy thoroughly. (3) Then there's the laughter of an unkind person when you want to disappear, and that person has cruelty to spare. (4) There's the laughter between friends during memories of your childhood antics.

WARM-UP EXERCISE: USING THE PARAGRAPH BLUEPRINT

Directions: Choose a topic for a paragraph that imitates the previous model paragraph about silence, and the imitation paragraph about laughter. Use one of these topics, or one of your own: sadness, happiness, success, disappointment, anger. Then, using the frame paragraph below as a blueprint, imitate the model paragraph. As a guide, use the **bolded** and <u>underlined</u> words in your imitation, but use your own words for the rest.

(1) **There are several kinds of** [YOUR TOPIC]. (2) **There's the** silence **of** being alone, **which** I like well enough. (3) **Then there's the** silence **of** one's father **when** you have nothing to say, **and** he has nothing to say. (4) **There's the** silence between you after the investigation of your stepmother's death.

In the following exercises, you'll imitate different kinds of paragraphs, but always building your sentences like the sentences in the model paragraph.

EXERCISE 2: IMITATING A FANTASY PARAGRAPH

Study each model paragraph and its twin paragraph, an imitation of the model paragraph. Pay close attention to how the sentences from both the model paragraph and the twin paragraph are built alike. Then write your own imitation, building your sentences like those in the model and its twin.

MODEL PARAGRAPH

(1) Once upon a time, a girl named September grew very tired indeed of her parents' house, where she washed the same teacups and gravy boats every day, slept on the same embroidered pillows, and played with the same small and amiable dog. (2) Because she had been born in May, and because she had a mole on her left cheek, and because her feet were very large and ungainly, the Green Wind took pity on her and flew to her window one evening just after her twelfth birthday. (3) He was dressed in a green smoking jacket and a green carriage-driver's cloak and green jodhpurs and green snowshoes. (4) It is very cold above the clouds in the shantytowns where the Six Winds live.

Catherynne M. Valente, *The Girl Who Circumnavigated Fairyland in a Ship of Her Own Making*

TALK ABOUT THESE QUESTIONS

1. What sentence tells three things September did?

2. What sentence has three sentence parts that begin with the word because?

3. What sentence tells why Green Wind wore warm clothing?

4. Which sentences use the word *and* lots of times?

TWIN PARAGRAPH

(1) Once upon a time a boy named Deacon got very excited indeed about his new school, where he read his fairy stories and fantastic poems every day, learned about new interesting constellations, and sang with the terrific musical and talented chorus. (2) Because he had been born too late, and because he had ugly scabs on both knees, and because his smile was very lopsided but contagious, the Sun Princess was interested in him and came to his room one night just after their first concert. (3) She was radiant in a golden silk gown and a golden fairy princess cloak and golden slippers and golden necklace. (4) It is very bright around the world in the neighborhoods where the Sun Princess hides.

IMITATING A PARAGRAPH ABOUT A FANTASY

Directions: Write an imitation of the model paragraph about a fantasy from your imagination, a TV show, a movie, a story, or a book. Each sentence from the model paragraph and the imitation paragraph is broken down into its sentence parts. The list of equivalent sentence parts will help you see how the sentence is built. Imitate one sentence part at a time for each sentence until you finish your imitation of the model paragraph.

Model Paragraph	Twin Paragraph
1a. Once upon a time,	**1a.** Once upon a time
1b. a girl named September	**1b.** a boy named Deacon
1c. grew very tired indeed of her parents' house,	**1c.** got very excited indeed about his new school,
1d. where she washed the same teacups and gravy boats every day,	**1d.** where he read his fairy stories and fantastic poems every day,
1e. slept on the same embroidered pillows,	**1e.** learned about new interesting constellations
1f. and played with the same small and amiable dog.	**1f.** and sang with the terrific musical and talented chorus.
2a. Because she had been born in May,	**2a.** Because he had been born too late,
2b. and because she had a mole on her left cheek,	**2b.** and because he had ugly scabs on both knees,
2c. and because her feet were very large and ungainly,	**2c.** and because his smile was very lopsided but contagious,
2d. the Green Wind took pity on her	**2d.** the Sun Princess was interested in him
2e. and flew to her window one evening	**2e.** and came to his room one night
2f. just after her twelfth birthday.	**2f.** just after their first concert.
3a. He was dressed in a green smoking jacket	**3a.** She was radiant in a golden silk gown
3b. and a green carriage-driver's cloak	**3b.** and a golden fairy princess cloak
3c. and green jodhpurs	**3c.** and golden slippers
3d. and green snowshoes.	**3d.** and golden necklace.
4a. It is very cold above the clouds	**4a.** It is very bright around the world
4b. in the shantytowns	**4b.** in the neighborhoods
4c. where the Six Winds live.	**4c.** where the Sun Princess appears.

EXERCISE 3: IMITATING A PARAGRAPH ABOUT A SPECIAL PLACE

MODEL PARAGRAPH

(1) It was the largest and most famous chocolate factory in the world! (2) It was Wonka's Factory, owned by a man called Mr. Willy Wonka, the greatest inventor and maker of chocolate that there has ever been. (3) What a tremendous, marvelous place it was! (4) It had huge iron gates leading in to it, and a high wall surrounding it, smoke belching from its chimneys, and strange whizzing sounds coming from deep inside it. (5) Outside the walls, for half a mile around in every direction, the air was scented with the heavy rich smell of melting chocolate.

Roald Dahl, *Charlie and the Chocolate Factory*

TALK ABOUT THESE QUESTIONS

1. Why do some sentences have exclamation marks?

2. What words describe the huge size of the chocolate factory?

3. Summarize how each sentence adds a new detail of the factory's huge size.

4. What are some emotions the paragraph makes readers feel?

TWIN PARAGRAPH

(1) It was the prettiest and most inviting small farm in the countryside! (2) It was a safe haven, run by a man named Mr. Harold Hartly, the kindest farmer and planter of crops that there had ever been. (3) What a happy, picturesque place it was! (4) It had whitewashed planked fences leading into it, and colorful azalea bushes surrounding it, fragrance wafting from its pasture, and many contented

cows wandering within meadows around the barn. (5) In every space, for almost a mile nearby with every view, the scene was filled with the lovely spring colors of blooming tulips.

IMITATING A PARAGRAPH ABOUT A SPECIAL PLACE

Directions: Write an imitation of the model paragraph about a special place from your life or your imagination, or from a TV show, movie, story, or book. Each sentence from the model paragraph and the imitation paragraph is broken down into its sentence parts. The list of equivalent sentence parts will help you see how the sentence is built. Imitate one sentence part at a time for each sentence until you finish your imitation of the model paragraph.

Model Paragraph	Twin Paragraph
1a. It was	**1a.** It was
1b. the largest and most famous chocolate factory	**1b.** the prettiest and most inviting small farm
1c. in the world!	**1c.** in the countryside!
2a. It was Wonka's Factory,	**2a.** It was a safe haven,
2b. owned by a man called Mr. Willy Wonka,	**2b.** run by a man named Mr. Harold Hartly,
2c. the greatest inventor and maker of chocolate	**2c.** the kindest farmer and planter of crops
2d. that there has ever been.	**2d.** that there had ever been.
3a. What a tremendous,	**3a.** What a happy,
3b. marvelous place	**3b.** picturesque place
3c. it was!	**3c.** it was!

4a. It had huge iron gates	**4a.** It had whitewashed planked fences
4b. leading in to it,	**4b.** leading in to it,
4c. and a high wall	**4c.** and colorful azalea bushes
4d. surrounding it,	**4d.** surrounding it,
4e. smoke belching from its chimneys,	**4e.** fragrance wafting from its pasture,
4f. and strange whizzing sounds	**4f.** and many contented cows
4g. coming from deep inside it.	**4g.** wandering within meadows around the barn.
5a. Outside the walls,	**5a.** In every space,
5b. for half a mile around	**5b.** for almost a mile nearby
5c. in every direction,	**5c.** with every view,
5d. the air was scented	**5d.** the scene was filled
5e. with the heavy rich smell	**5e.** with the lovely spring colors
5f. of melting chocolate.	**5f.** of blooming tulips.

EXERCISE 4: IMITATING A PARAGRAPH ABOUT SOMETHING YOU WANT

MODEL PARAGRAPH

(1) He always wanted horses. (2) He didn't know why, but he just liked them. (3) He liked the way they looked, the way they moved, the way they smelled. (4) He could watch horses for hours. (5) There was something beautiful about the way they stood motionless in the sun, one hoof cocked up. (6) He liked the curve of a horses' foot, the delicate way they never stepped on a giddy chicken or a small child. (7) He liked their neighing and nickering. (8) He had never had horses, and he didn't know how to ride one, and he didn't know what it would

take to keep them, but when he ended up with a place that had a barn and some ground, he decided to try the company of horses.

Alan Armstrong, *Whittington*

TALK ABOUT THESE QUESTIONS

1. What word begins most of the sentences?

2. How does the first sentence preview the paragraph?

3. What three-letter word connects two sentences in sentence 2?

4. Removing three words in sentence 8 would create three separate sentences. What are those three words? <u>Hint</u>: Each word has three letters. What puncutation mark would then replace all three commas?

TWIN PARAGRAPH

(1) Tricialouise thoroughly enjoyed her kitten. (2) She certainly knew why, and she just adored it. (3) She loved the way it purred, the way it snuggled, the way it felt. (4) She could pet her kitten for hours. (5) There was something irresistible about the way the kitten lay curled in the chair, its head tucked sideways. (6) She loved the feel of her kitten's paw, the gentle touch it always gave to her outstretched hand or a tickling finger. (7) She loved its meowing and purring. (8) She had always had a kitten, and Tricialouise certainly knew how to live with one, and she didn't know what it would be to lose one, so when she grew up with a husband who had no kittens and some reluctance, she tried to demonstrate the magic of kittens.

IMITATING A PARAGRAPH ABOUT SOMETHING YOU WANT

Directions: Write an imitation of the model paragraph about something you have always wanted. Each sentence from the model paragraph and the imitation paragraph is broken down into its sentence parts. The list of equivalent sentence parts will help you see how the sentence is built. Imitate one sentence part at a time for each sentence until you finish your imitation of the model paragraph.

Model Paragraph	Twin Paragraph
1a. He **1b.** always wanted horses.	**1a.** Tricialouise **1b.** thoroughly enjoyed her kitten.
2a. He **2b.** didn't know why, **2c.** but he just liked them.	**2a.** She **2b.** certainly knew why, **2c.** and she just adored it.
3a. He liked **3b.** the way they looked, **3c.** the way they moved, **3d.** the way they smelled.	**3a.** She loved **3b.** the way it purred, **3c.** the way it snuggled, **3d.** the way it felt.
4a. He **4b.** could watch horses **4c.** for hours.	**4a.** She **4b.** could pet her kitten **4c.** for hours.
5a. There was something beautiful **5b.** about the way **5c.** they stood motionless **5d.** in the sun, **5e.** one hoof cocked up.	**5a.** There was something irresistible **5b.** about the way **5c.** the kitten lay curled **5d.** in the chair, **5e.** its head tucked sideways.
6a. He liked the curve of a horses' foot, **6b.** the delicate way **6c.** they never stepped on a giddy chicken **6d.** or a small child.	**6a.** She loved the feel of her kitten's paw, **6b.** the gentle touch **6c.** it always gave to her outstretched hand **6d.** or a tickling finger.

7a. He liked	**7a.** She loved
7b. their neighing	**7b.** its meowing
7c. and nickering.	**7c.** and purring.
8a. He had never had horses,	**8a.** She had always had a kitten,
8b. and he didn't know how to ride on one,	**8b.** and Tricialouise certainly knew how to live with one,
8c. and he didn't know	**8c.** and she didn't know
8d. what it would take to keep them,	**8d.** what it would be to lose one,
8e. but when he ended up	**8e.** so when she grew up
8f. with a place	**8f.** with a husband
8g. that had a barn and some ground,	**8g.** who had no kittens and some reluctance,
8h. he decided to try the company of horses.	**8h.** she tried to demonstrate the magic of kittens.

EXERCISE 5: IMITATING A PARAGRAPH ABOUT SOMETHING TERRIFYING

MODEL PARAGRAPH

(1) It was a dark and stormy night. (2) In her attic bedroom, Meg, wrapped in an old patchwork quilt, sat on the foot of her bed and watched the trees tossing in the frenzied lashing of the wind. (3) Behind the trees, clouds scudded frantically across the sky. (4) Every few moments, the moon ripped through them, creating ghostly shadows that raced across the ground. (5) The house shook. (6) Wrapped in her quilt, Meg shook. (7) The window rattled madly in the wind, and she pulled the quilt close about her. (8) Her shivering grew uncontrollable.

Madeleine L'Engle, *A Wrinkle in Time* (adapted)

TALK ABOUT THESE QUESTIONS

1. Why is the first sentence (the preview sentence) a good beginning?

2. What sights outside Meg's window frighten her?

3. What sound increases Meg's terror?

4. Why is the last sentence a good ending?

TWIN PARAGRAPH

(1) It was a small and insistent noise. (2) In his upstairs room, Larry, finished with his math homework, rose from the comfort of his chair and heard the sound moving across the back porch of his house. (3) Around the porch, furniture moved abruptly near the door. (4) Every few seconds, the sound moved under him, making mysterious thumpings that sounded like an intruder. (5) The noise increased. (6) Paralyzed in his room, Larry panicked. (7) The thumping penetrated steadily through the door, and he felt a chill deep inside him. (8) His fear became unbearable.

IMITATING A PARAGRAPH ABOUT A TERRIFYING EXPERIENCE

Directions: Write an imitation of the model paragraph about a terrifying experience from your life or your imagination, or from a TV show, movie, story, or book. Each sentence from the model paragraph and the imitation paragraph is broken down into its sentence parts. The list of equivalent sentence parts will help you see how the sentence is built. Imitate one sentence part at a time for each sentence until you finish your imitation of the model paragraph.

Model Paragraph	Twin Paragraph
1a. It	**1a.** It
1b. was	**1b.** was
1c. a dark and stormy night.	**1c.** a small and insistent noise.
2a. In her attic bedroom,	**2a.** In his upstairs room,
2b. Meg,	**2b.** Larry,
2c. wrapped in an old patchwork quilt,	**2c.** finished with his math homework,
2d. sat on the foot of her bed	**2d.** rose from the comfort of his chair
2e. and watched the trees	**2e.** and heard the sound
2f. tossing in the frenzied lashing of the wind.	**2f.** moving across the back porch of his house.
3a. Behind the trees,	**3a.** Around the porch,
3b. clouds scudded frantically	**3b.** furniture moved abruptly
3c. across the sky.	**3c.** near the door.
4a. Every few moments,	**4a.** Every few seconds,
4b. the moon ripped through them,	**4b.** the sound moved under him,
4c. creating ghostly shadows	**4c.** making mysterious thumpings
4d. that raced across the ground.	**4d.** that sounded like an intruder.
5a. The house	**5a.** The noise
5b. shook.	**5b.** increased.
6a. Wrapped in her quilt,	**6a.** Paralyzed in his room,
6b. Meg	**6b.** Larry
6c. shook.	**6c.** panicked.
7a. The window rattled madly	**7a.** The thumping penetrated steadily
7b. in the wind,	**7b.** through the door,
7c. and she pulled the quilt	**7c.** and he felt a chill
7d. close about her.	**7d.** deep inside him.

| **8a.** Her shivering | **8a.** His fear |
| **8b.** grew uncontrollable. | **8b.** became unbearable. |

PARAGRAPH WORKOUT

Written by famous authors, the model paragraphs that follow are the opening paragraphs of stories. Study the model paragraphs to learn how the authors make readers want to continue the story. Then choose one model to imitate for an opening paragraph of your own story. You are writing only the first paragraph for your story, but your paragraph may turn out so well that you will keep working on it to finish your story.

MODEL PARAGRAPH ONE

(1) There is no lake in Camp Green Lake. (2) There once was a large lake there, the largest lake in Texas. (3) That was over a hundred years ago. (4) Now it is just a dry, flat wasteland.

Louis Sachar, *Holes*

MODEL PARAGRAPH TWO

(1) He waited on the stoop until twilight, pretending to watch the sun melt into the dirty gray Harlem sky. (2) Up and down the street, car stereos were on and blared into the sour air. (3) Men dragged out card tables, laughing. (4) Cars cruised through the garbage and broken glass, older guys showing off their Friday night girls.

Robert Lipsyte, *The Contender*

MODEL PARAGRAPH THREE

(1) The notes were appearing everywhere. (2) Everyone was talking about it. (3) The first time Harriet and Beth Ellen ever saw anyone get one was one day in July when they were in the supermarket in Water

Mill. (4) They were standing at the checkout counter waiting to pay for their cookies. (5) The woman with mean eyes who always checked them out was getting ready to charge them, when she suddenly drew her hand back from the cash register as though bitten by a snake.

Louise Fitzhugh, *The Long Secret*

MODEL PARAGRAPH FOUR

(1) Long ago, on the wild and windy isle of Berk, a smallish Viking with a longish name stood up to his ankles in snow. (2) Hiccup Horrendous Haddock the Third, the Hope and Heir to the Tribe of the Hairy Hooligans, had been feeling slightly sick ever since he woke up that morning. (3) Ten boys, including Hiccup, were hoping to become full members of the Tribe by passing the Dragon Initiation Program. (4) They were standing on a bleak little beach at the bleakest spot on the whole bleak island. (5) A heavy snow was falling.

Cressida Cowell, *How to Train Your Dragon*

MODEL PARAGRAPH FIVE

(1) I clasped the flask between my hands even though the warmth from the tea had long since leached into the frozen air. (2) My muscles were clenched tight against the cold. (3) If a pack of wild dogs were to appear at this moment, the odds of scaling a tree before they attacked were not in my favor. (4) I should have got up, moved around, and worked the stiffness from my limbs. (5) Instead I sat, as motionless as the rock beneath me, while the dawn began to lighten the woods. (6) I couldn't fight the sun. (7) I could only watch helplessly as it dragged me into a day that I've been dreading for months.

Suzanne Collins, *Catching Fire* (adapted)

REVIEW

You learn lots of things by watching people do them: riding a bike, swinging a bat, combing hair, tying a tie, making a bed, and so forth. You have watched lots of authors writing sentences and paragraphs and then imitated what they did to build your sentences and paragraphs like theirs.

PREVIEW

You learned earlier how to unscramble sentence messes. Now learn to unscramble paragraph messes. Always tidy up messes—in your sentences, in your paragraphs, and, for sure, in your room.

UNSCRAMBLING PARAGRAPHS

In the paragraph below, sentence parts and sentences are scrambled. Readers see a mess of nonsense. In the unscrambled version, sentence parts and sentences are properly arranged, so readers can easily understand the paragraph.

SCRAMBLED PARAGRAPH

(1) Drumming her fingernails saw a woman on the table I also over and over. (2) I in a brown, linty suit large-shouldered man saw a. (3) A flower in her hair happened to have she. (4) Him uncomfortable it looked like it made. (5) How they look to strangers to look at one's family it is curious and try to imagine. (6) Was like a tin horse's galloping the sound. (7) Particularly the man were both smiling they. (8) My parents at the people I looked who were with me.

If you said, "Whew! Who wrote that? That doesn't even make sense," you're right. Now try this version, with sentence parts and sentences unscrambled to create the original paragraph.

UNSCRAMBLED PARAGRAPH

(1) I looked at the people who were with me, my parents. (2) It is curious to look at one's family and try to imagine how they look to strangers. (3) I saw a large-shouldered man in a brown, linty suit. (4) It looked like it made him uncomfortable. (5) I also saw a woman drumming her fingernails on the table, over and over. (6) The sound was like a tin horse's galloping. (7) She happened to have a flower in her hair. (8) They were both smiling, particularly the man.

Lemony Snicket, *Who Could That Be at This Hour?*

The two versions have exactly the same words, but the scrambled version is almost meaningless, a jumbled mess, while the unscrambled version is meaningful, a description of the young person's parents as strangers would see them.

In good sentences, like those in the unscrambled version, sentence parts have a clear link to each other. In good paragraphs, sentences also have a clear link to each other. The following exercises focus on clear links of sentence parts within sentences, and of sentences within paragraphs. In your own sentences and paragraphs, have clear links to prevent a jumbled mess.

EXERCISE 1: UNSCRAMBLING SENTENCE PARTS

Underneath each sentence from the paragraph are scrambled sentence parts from the original sentence. Add them to the sentence where they make sense.

Note: Use capital letters for the beginning of sentences, and commas for pauses.

PARAGRAPH ONE (from *A Little Princess* by Frances Hodgson Burnett)

Summary: *A doll, Sara's favorite toy, is described.*

1. The doll had certainly a very intelligent expression.

   a. when Sara took her in her arms

   b. in her eyes

2. She was a large doll.

   a. to carry about easily

   b. but not too large

3. She had naturally curling golden-brown hair, and her eyes were a deep, clear, grey blue.

   a. and not mere painted lines

   b. with soft, thick eyelashes

c. which were real eyelashes

d. which hung like a mantle about her

PARAGRAPH TWO (from *Who Could That Be at This Hour?* by Lemony Snicket)

Summary: *A dirty restaurant with terrible food is described.*

1. The Hemlock Tearoom and Stationery Shop is a place.
    a. even when they are clean

    b. where the floors always feel dirty

2. They were not clean.
    a. in question

    b. on the day

3. The food at the Hemlock is too awful to eat.
    a. including those on exhibit at the Museum of Bad Breakfast

    b. which are probably the worst eggs in the entire city

    c. particularly the eggs

    d. where visitors can learn just how badly eggs can be prepared

PARAGRAPH THREE (from *The Mouse and the Motorcycle* by Beverly Cleary)

Summary: *A hotel employee named Matt helps a mother, father, and their son.*

1. Keith did not know he was being watched.
    a. as he entered Room 215 of the Mountain View Inn

    b. the boy in the rumpled shorts and shirt

2. Neither did two others.

    a. who both looked hot and tired

    b. his mother and father

3. The fourth person entering Room 215 was Matt.

    a. was the bellboy

    b. who

    c. at the moment

    d. sixty years old

4. Matt did everything.

    a. and sometimes preventing children from hitting one another

    b. other times

    c. who telephoned room service to order food sent to their rooms

    d. with croquet mallets on the lawn behind the hotel

    e. carrying trays for people

    f. replacing worn out light bulbs, renewing washers in leaky faucets

PARAGRAPH FOUR (from *Crispin: The Cross of Lead* by Avi)

Summary: *A young boy fleeing an evil man runs frantically into the forest.*

1. I paid no mind into what I ran

    a. or the roof of trees above

    b. tore on brambles and bushes

    c. or that my sole garment

    d. barely aware of the earth beneath my feet

    e. a gray wool tunic

2. Nor did I care.
   a. causing me to fall

   b. kept tripping me

   c. that my leather shoes

   d. catching on roots or stones

3. I picked myself up.
   a. panting, crying

   b. and rushed on

   c. each time

4. Deeper and deeper into the ancient woods I went.
   a. my head striking a stone

   b. and fell again

   c. until I tripped

   d. past thick bracken and stately oaks

5. I lay upon the decaying earth
   a. fingers clutching rotting leaves

   b. a cold rain drenching me

   c. stunned

6. I was entombed.
   a. in a world

   b. as daylight faded

   c. darker than any night could bring

PARAGRAPH FIVE (from *Sara, Plain and Tall* by Patricia MacLachlan)

Summary: *A family is saddened by the death of the mother.*

1. The prairie reached out.

    a. where the sky came down

    b. outside

    c. and touched the places

2. There were patches of snow.

    a. everywhere

    b. and ice

    c. though the winter was nearly over

3. I looked at the long dirt road.

    a. cruel and sunny

    b. that Mama died

    c. that crawled across the plains

    d. remembering the morning

4. They had come for her

    a. in a wagon

    b. to be buried

    c. and taken her away

5. The cousins and aunts and uncles came

    a. then

    b. but couldn't

    c. and tried to fill up the house

6. They left.

    a. one by one

    b. slowly

7. The days seemed long

    a. even though it wasn't winter

    b. afterwards

    c. with Papa never singing

    d. and dark like winter days

EXERCISE 2: UNSCRAMBLING SENTENCE PARTS AND SENTENCES

First, unscramble the <u>sentence parts</u> to produce a good sentence. Next, unscramble the <u>sentences</u> to make a good paragraph. Write out and punctuate the paragraph. Write your unscrambled sentences on paper strips (or a computer) to make it easier to arrange your unscrambled sentences into a good paragraph.

Note: Use capital letters for the beginning of sentences, and commas for pauses.

    Scrambled Paragraph One: When you unscramble it, the paragraph will describe a hairy character named Spook.

        Joseph Delaney, *The Last Apprentice*

1a. the same color

1b. his eyes

1c. as my own

1d. were green

2a. sprouting out of his nostrils

2b. of black hair

2c. too

2d. there was quite a bit

3a. matched his beard

3b. the hair sticking out

3c. which was gray

3d. from under the front of the Spook's hood

3e. and very bushy

3f. but his eyebrows were black

> *Scrambled Paragraph Two:* When you unscramble it, the
> paragraph will describe a batter ready for the pitch.
> Clair Bee, *Strike Three!*

1a. as he slowly got to his feet

1b. it was a clumsy fall

1c. the boy's face burning

2a. the tall pitcher on the mound

2b. Chip stepped up

2c. of the home plate

2d. to the side

2e. over his short hair

2f. yanked his cap a little farther down

2g. and eyed Trullo

3a. a long, questioning look

3b. picked up the bat

3c. and gave Trullo

3d. he

4a. Chip

4b. and landed

4c. from the ball

4d. fell away

4e. in the dirt

5a. and then blazed a fast one

5b. began his windup

5c. straight for Chip's head

5d. Trullo

> ***Scrambled Paragraph Three:*** When you unscramble it, the paragraph will explain how a spider web's center is like the pupil of an eye.
>
> Ursula K. LeGuin, *Earthsea: The Farthest Shore*

1a. a circle delicately suspended

1b. a spider had spun a web

1c. between two tall grass blades in the clearing

2a. seemed to watch them both

2b. with its black center

2c. the round web

3a. it was

3b. the pupil of an eye

3c. no larger than

3d. a grey and black thing

4a. the spider waited

4b. as in the center

4c. were catching the sunlight

4d. the silver threads

> ***Scrambled Paragraph Four:*** When you unscramble it, the paragraph will describe a young boy on a ship during a dangerous storm.
>
> Walter Farley, *The Black Stallion*

1a. on him

1b. of feet stepping

1c. became conscious

1d. then Alec

2a. resounded on the water

2b. zigzagging through the sky

2c. never diminishing

2d. the sharp cracks of lightning

3a. was gone

3b. the sailor

3c. when it had passed

4a. yelling and screaming

4b. and crawling over him

4c. the passengers

4d. were climbing

5a. to hold on to the rail

5b. one of the crew

5c. Alec saw

5d. desperately fighting

5e. make his way along the deck

6a. for what seemed hours

6b. yet somehow

6c. the ship plowed through wave after wave

6d. trembling and careening on its side

6e. managing to stay afloat

7a. the ship rolled sideways

7b. swept over the boat

7c. and a huge wave

> ***Scrambled Paragraph Five:*** When you unscramble it, the
> paragraph will describe how dwarfs during a landslide slid down a
> slope.
>
> J. R. R. Tolkien, *The Hobbit*

1a. that saved them

1b. it was the trees

1c. at the bottom

2a. before long

2b. on the move

2c. above them and below them

2d. the whole slope seemed

3a. were at the top

3b. the remains of a landslide

3c. of a wide steep slope

3d. the dwarfs

3e. of fallen stones

4a. of the trunks

4b. some dwarfs caught hold

4c. from the onslaught of the rocks

4d. and swung themselves into lower branches

4e. and some got behind a tree for shelter

5a. were disturbed and bounded off

5b. with a dust and a noise

5c. crashing down

5d. then lumps of rock

6a. the dwarfs were sliding away

6b. of slipping slabs and stones

6c. in a fearful confusion

6d. huddled all together

7a. went clattering down

7b. soon larger bits

7c. of split stone

7d. slithering and rolling

7e. and started other stones

8a. rubbish and small pebbles

8b. to go down those remains

8c. rolled away from their feet

8d. when they began

PARAGRAPH WORKOUT

Good paragraphs have detailed information. For any paragraph you wrote earlier, add more details by doing these steps.

- Read your paragraph several times to find places <u>within sentences</u> where you could add new *sentence parts* for more information. Then, also find places <u>between sentences</u> where you could add new *sentences* for more information.

- Add one or more sentence parts to at least three of your sentences. For examples of kinds of sentence parts you could add, look back at the exercises in this section.

- Add three new *sentences* to your paragraph for more detail, information, and interest.

- Give your revised paragraph a creative title, and share your new paragraph with other students.

REVIEW

Scrambling, for eggs, is good, but for sentences and paragraphs creates messy meanings. Arrange the words in your sentences, and the sentences in your paragraphs clearly and effectively so that your readers can read them easily.

PREVIEW

Egg dishes come in different kinds, not just scrambled. Paragraphs come in different kinds, too. Next, you will study and write six different kinds.

PUTTING PARAGRAPHS TO WORK

People have different jobs because lots of different jobs need doing. Paragraphs have different jobs, too, because lots of different ideas need telling. After reading each example paragraph that follows, write a paragraph with the same job and purpose. Build your sentences like the sentences in the authors' paragraphs by using lots of sentence-composing tools for detail and dazzle in your own paragraph.

EXERCISE 1: NARRATIVE PARAGRAPH

A narrative paragraph's job is <u>to tell a true or a made-up story</u>. In this example of a narrative paragraph, the author tells the story of two boys playing cards.

EXAMPLE

(1) Jamie and his buddy Bruce played cards on the bus. (2) Each day meant a continuation of the day before. (3) The game was nothing very complicated, nothing terribly refined. (4) They played "War," that simple game where each player puts down a card, and the higher card takes both. (5) If the cards are the same, there is a war which involves putting down more cards. (6) Winner then takes all the war cards. (7) Every night when Bruce got off at his stop, he'd take his stack of cards home with him. (8) Jamie would do the same. (9) They always took a vow not to shuffle. (10) At the stop before Bruce's house, they would stop playing, wrap a rubber band around each pile, hold the stack under each other's chin, and spit on each other's deck to vow that they would not shuffle the cards. (11) Then each boy tapped his deck and put it in his pocket. (12) Claudia, Jamie's older sister, found the whole procedure disgusting.

E. L. Konigsburg, *From the Mixed-Up Files of*
Mrs. Basil E. Frankweiler

YOUR TURN

Tell the story of an event from your life or from the life of someone you know, or make up a story from your imagination. End your narrative paragraph with a memorable sentence, as in the example paragraph.

Important: Within your narrative paragraph, use a variety of sentence-composing tools to build a strong paragraph similar to the preceding example paragraph.

EXERCISE 2: INFORMATIVE PARAGRAPH

An informative paragraph's job is to educate the reader about a particular topic. This example informative paragraph illustrates how the seas around us change in unpredictable ways.

EXAMPLE

(1) All through the long history of Earth the sea has been an area of unrest where waves have broken heavily against the land, and where the tides have receded, and then returned. (2) For no two successive days is the shore line precisely the same. (3) Not only do the tides advance and retreat in their eternal rhythms, but the level of the sea itself is never at rest. (4) It rises or falls as the glaciers melt or grow, as the floor of the deep ocean basins shifts under its increasing load of sediments, or as the earth's crust along the continental margins warps up or down in adjustment to strain and tension. (5) Today a little more land may belong to the sea, tomorrow a little less. (6) Always the edge of the sea remains an elusive and indefinable boundary.

Rachel Carson, *The Edge of the Sea*

YOUR TURN

Write an informative paragraph about how storms happen: for example, a tornado, a hurricane, a lightning strike, a tsunami, or some other devastating natural event. Research your topic before drafting your paragraph to learn more about that particular kind of storm. Finish your paragraph emphasizing a point made in your paragraph, as in the example paragraph.

Important: Within your informative paragraph, use a variety of sentence-composing tools to build a strong paragraph similar to the example paragraph above.

EXERCISE 3: DESCRIPTIVE PARAGRAPH

A descriptive paragraph's job is to create a picture in the reader's mind. In this example of a descriptive paragraph, the narrator describes a particular grave where a ghoul lurks.

EXAMPLE

(1) One grave in every graveyard belongs to the ghouls. (2) Wander any graveyard long enough, and you will find it, water-stained and bulging, with cracked or broken stone, scraggly grass or rank weeds about it, and a feeling when you reach it of abandonment. (3) It may be colder than the other gravestones, too, and the name on the stone is all too often impossible to read. (4) If there is a statue on the grave, it will be headless or so scabbed with fungus and lichens as to look like a fungus itself. (5) If the grave makes you want to be somewhere else, that is the ghoul-gate. (6) There is one in every graveyard.

Neil Gaiman, *The Graveyard Book*

YOUR TURN

Write a descriptive paragraph about an unusual place: a junkyard, an overgrown lot, an abandoned house, an alley, a theme park, a zoo, or someplace else. Begin your paragraph with a sentence that previews the place, as in the model. Describe all the details that make the place unusual.

Also, end your paragraph with a sentence that summarizes the paragraph, as in the example paragraph.

<u>Important</u>: Within your descriptive paragraph, use a variety of sentence-composing tools to build a strong paragraph similar to the example paragraph above.

EXERCISE 4: EXPLANATORY PARAGRAPH

An explanatory paragraph's job is <u>to explain an idea or fact</u>. This example of an explanatory paragraph tells why certain grasshoppers are eaten by birds, but others are not.

EXAMPLE

(1) The bright green grasshoppers are just too easy to spot. (2) The birds spend their days gobbling them up while the yellow grasshoppers hide nearby and taunt their less-fortunate brothers. (3) The grasshoppers that are born a bit yellower to begin with live to an old age in the drought because the birds can't see them in the parched grass. (4) The greener ones, the ones the birds pick off, don't last long enough to grow big. (5) Only the yellower ones survive because they are more fit to survive in the torrid weather, hidden by the parched yellowed grass.

Jacqueline Kelly, *The Evolution of Calpurnia Tate*

YOUR TURN

Write an explanatory paragraph that explains something in nature: light in a lightning bug, transformation of a caterpillar into a butterfly, change of leaf color in the fall, reemergence of flowers from bulbs in the spring, or something else. First research that process to learn more about how it works. Finish the paragraph with a sentence summarizing the process, as in the example paragraph.

Important: Within your explanatory paragraph, use a variety of sentence-composing tools to build a strong paragraph similar to the example paragraph above.

EXERCISE 5: DEFINITION PARAGRAPH

A definition paragraph's job is <u>to tell what something is</u>, often by giving several examples. This example of a definition paragraph describes what death was like in the character's personal experience.

EXAMPLE

(1) No one had ever told him exactly what would happen if anyone caught him. (2) Maybe it would be death. (3) Death was what happened to the runt pigs who got stepped on by their stronger brothers and sisters. (4) Death was a fly that stopped buzzing when the swatter hit it. (5) He had a hard time thinking about himself in connection with the smashed fly or the dead pig, going stiff in the sun. (6) It made his stomach feel funny even trying.

Margaret Peterson Haddix, *Among the Hidden*

YOUR TURN

Write a definition paragraph that gives several personal examples from your life of what you are defining: strength, happiness, humor, love, poverty, war, childhood—or choose something else. Finish the paragraph with a sentence giving a personal response to what you define, as in the example paragraph.

Important: Within your definition paragraph, use a variety of sentence-composing tools to build a strong paragraph similar to the example paragraph above.

EXERCISE 6: PERSUASIVE PARAGRAPH

A persuasive paragraph's job is <u>to convince your readers to agree with you</u>. This example of a persuasive paragraph argues for changes in how violence is presented in the media and how viewers can help to solve the problem of excessive violence in entertainment.

EXAMPLE

> (1) The entertainment industry can help our troubled children by cutting back on the number of violent portrayals, by making them less graphic and attention-getting, and by emphasizing the sorrowful consequences of violence rather than glamorizing and making heroes of violent men. (2) We must become more discriminating viewers and stop watching violent programs. (3) We must enter into dialogue with the industry, thanking studios and networks for every good offering and supporting them at the box office and in the ratings races. (4) We must support the sponsors of good programs and protest irresponsible companies of bad programs.
>
> Barbara Hattemer, "Media and Our Youth"

YOUR TURN

Write a persuasive paragraph that gives several reasons readers should agree with your opinion about a controversial issue. Finish the paragraph with a sentence summarizing what you want your readers to do, as in the example paragraph.

<u>Important</u>: Within your persuasive paragraph, use a variety of sentence-composing tools to build a strong paragraph similar to the example paragraph.

REVIEW

Congratulations on putting sentences and paragraphs in their proper places. You also learned the various jobs and purposes of paragraphs, and put those to work in your own paragraphs.

PREVIEW

You're almost finished, but the big test is next. You will use everything you've learned. Now you'll build your sentences and paragraphs stronger than ever by adding pizzazz!

ADDING PIZZAZZ

Power results from strength. Power tools result from a motor's strength. A power saw is easier to use than a handsaw because the motor's strength is greater than the hand's strength.

At the beginning of this worktext, you learned the two basic requirements for a sentence: subject and predicate. You then learned how to go far beyond the subject and predicate by adding sentence-composing power tools to your sentences to build stronger paragraphs.

Look at more evidence of tool power. Read these paragraphs from winners of the Newberry Medal, an annual honor for the best book for young readers. The "before" paragraphs lack tools. The "after" paragraphs include them.

EXAMPLES OF TOOL POWER

Paragraph One: *Hector cannot understand why his appearance isn't as attractive as his sister's.*

Before Tools: Hector's sister Rowanne was upstairs in her bedroom. Hector could hear her humming. He was crossing the front hall on his way to the kitchen and he glanced and gave himself a little smile. This time he smiled at himself. It struck him as an improvement on the usual averageness of his face. An aura of interestingness his sister's face had all the time, but his did not. They both had auburn hair, but Hector's shot out from his head in wiry, dissenting clumps.

After Tools: **Meanwhile,** Hector's sister Rowanne was upstairs in her bedroom, **changing her clothes or something**. Hector could hear her humming, **the sound of drawers opening and closing**. He was crossing the front hall on his way to the kitchen and, **as he passed the mirror**, he glanced and gave himself a little smile, **something he always did, for encouragement, maybe**. This time he smiled at himself, **just as a slanted ray of sun shot through one of the diamond-shaped windows in the front door at the side of**

his face, producing a sort of side-lit, golden disembodied-head
effect in the mirror**. It struck him as an improvement on the usual
averageness of his face, **adding some drama, some intrigue**. An aura
of interestingness his sister's face had all the time, but his did not,
**which mystified him because when he compared their features
one at a time, a lot of them seemed identical, or almost identical,
except their hair**. They both had auburn hair, but, **while Rowanne's
auburn hair plummeted in a serene, graceful waterfall to her waist**,
Hector's shot out from his head in wiry, dissenting clumps.

Lynne Rae Perkins, *Criss Cross*

Paragraph Two: *A young girl named Lucky learns why Short Sammy
gave up drinking.*

Before Tools: Lucky Trimble crouched. She listened as Short Sammy
told his story. Short Sammy's story was still her favorite. Sammy told
of the day when he had drunk half a gallon of rum listening to Johnny
Cash all morning in his parked '62 Cadillac. Lucky lifted the way-too-
curly hair off her neck. She noticed two small black birds nearby. Lucky
put her ear to the hole. Short Sammy veered off and told about the old
days when he was broke and couldn't afford to buy rum.

After Tools: **In a wedge of shade behind the Dumpster,** Lucky
Trimble crouched. **Her ear near a hole in the paint-chipped wall
of Hard Pan's Found Object Wind Chime Museum and Visitor
Center,** she listened as Short Sammy told his story: **how he hit rock
bottom, how he quit drinking and found his Higher Power.** Short
Sammy's story, **of all the rock-bottom stories Lucky had heard
at twelve-step anonymous meetings—alcoholics, gamblers,
smokers, and overeaters—**was still her favorite. Sammy told of the
day when he had drunk half a gallon of rum listening to Johnny Cash
all morning in his parked '62 Cadillac, **falling out of the car when he
saw a rattlesnake in the passenger seat biting his dog Roy on the**

scrotum. **With her hand above the little hole that Short Sammy's voice was coming out of,** Lucky lifted the way-too-curly hair off her neck. She noticed two small black birds nearby, **panting like dogs from the heat, their beaks open, their feathers puffed up. Because Sammy's voice always got low and soft when he came to the tragical end of the story,** Lucky put her ear to the hole. **To stretch the story out and get more suspense going for the big ending,** Short Sammy veered off and told about the old days when he was broke and couldn't afford to buy rum, **making homemade liquor from cereal box raisins and any kind of fruit he could scrounge up.**

Susan Patron, *The Higher Power of Lucky* (adapted)

Paragraph Three: *During a musical performance, Jeffrey thinks of a way to get his aunt and uncle to communicate with each other.*

Before Tools: Jeffrey probably started screaming from the start of the song, but nobody knew it because he was drowned out by all the other voices. Then the music ended, and Jeffrey went right on screaming. The music director faced the singers. Faces began to change. There was a quick smattering of giggling by some people. Then the giggling stopped, and eyes started to shift, and heads started to turn.

After Tools: Jeffrey probably started screaming from the start of the song, **which was "Talk to the Animals,"** but nobody knew it because he was drowned out by all the other voices. Then the music ended, and Jeffrey went right on screaming, **his face bright red by now, his neck bulging.** The music director faced the singers, **frozen with his arms still raised. In the audience,** faces began to change. There was a quick smattering of giggling by some people, **who figured the screaming kid was some part of the show, some funny animal maybe.** Then the giggling stopped, and eyes started to shift, and heads started to turn, **because now everybody could see that this wasn't part of the show**

at all, that little Jeffrey McGee wasn't supposed to be up there on the risers, pointing to his aunt and uncle, bellowing out from the midst of the chorus, "Talk! Talk, will ya! Talk! Talk! Talk! Talk!"

Jerry Spinelli, *Maniac McGee*

Those sentence-composing power tools add valuable extras to the sentences of paragraphs. Here's why. The best cars have lots of extras to attract buyers, additions like great sound systems, stunning wheels, leather seats, remote starters, and so forth. The best pizzas have lots of toppings to satisfy customers, fixings like pepperoni or sausage or peppers or hamburger or onions or olives or shrimp. The best paragraphs, and the sentences they contain, also have extras to attract readers, sentence parts and sentences that add useful details and information. Accessories are to cars what elaboration is to writing. For cars or paragraphs (and pizzas, too), additions create a much better product. In these final exercises, you'll use sentence-composing tools to create paragraph pizzazz—a style that dazzles.

EXERCISE 1: PLACING ADDITIONS

Underneath each sentence of the paragraph are additions that appear in the author's original paragraph. Insert the additions where they are most effective. The sentences are in the correct order, but the additions are scrambled.

Note: Use capital letters for the beginning of sentences, and commas for pauses.

PARAGRAPH ONE (from *Little House on the Prairie* by Laura Ingalls Wilder)

What is the paragraph about? A pioneer family with three young children abandons their home to travel to a new home. Here's the stripped-down paragraph. Without tools, the paragraph is really *forgettable*.

Without Pizzazz: Pa and Ma and Mary and Laura and Baby Carrie left their little house. They drove away.

With Pizzazz: Now insert the additions, and notice their power to add pizzazz to the paragraph. With tools, the paragraph is very *moving*.

----

1. Pa and Ma and Mary and Laura and Baby Carrie left their little house.

    a. when all the grandfathers and grandmothers of today were

    b. or perhaps not even born

    c. a long time ago

    d. little boys and little girls or very small babies

    e. in the Big Woods of Wisconsin

2. They drove away.

    a. among the big trees

    b. leaving it lonely and empty

    c. never to see that little house again

    d. in the clearing

PARAGRAPH TWO (from *The Wonderful Wizard of Oz* by L. Frank Baum)

What is the paragraph about? Dorothy and her aunt and uncle live in a small house with a cellar for protection during windstorms. Here's the stripped-down paragraph. Without tools, the paragraph is totally *forgettable*.

Without Pizzazz: Dorothy lived in the midst of the great Kansas prairies. Their house was small. The cellar was a small hole dug in the ground. It was reached by a trap-door.

With Pizzazz: Now insert the additions, and notice their power to add pizzazz to the paragraph. With tools, the paragraph is clearly *vivid*.

----

1. Dorothy lived in the midst of the great Kansas prairies.

   a. who was a farmer

   b. and Aunt Em

   c. who was the farmer's wife

   d. with Uncle Henry

2. Their house was small.

   a. had to be carried

   b. to build it

   c. for the lumber

   d. by wagon many miles

3. The cellar was a small hole dug in the ground.

   a. where the family could go

   b. a cyclone cellar

   c. to crush any building in its path

   d. mighty enough

   e. if one of those great whirlwinds arose

4. It was reached by a trap-door.

   a. into the small, dark hole

   b. from which a ladder

   c. led down

PARAGRAPH THREE (from *The Land of Stories:*
The Wishing Well **by Chris Colfer)**

What is the paragraph about? Near midnight, a mysterious woman slowly descends a dungeon's steps into a prison. Here's the stripped-down paragraph. Without tools, it's not very *scary*.

> **Without Pizzazz:** Large rats chased each other across the floor. All was quiet. A single set of footsteps echoed throughout the halls. A young woman emerged down the steps. She made her way past the row of cells. Her pace became slower and slower.

> **With Pizzazz:** Now insert the additions, and notice their power to add pizzazz to the paragraph. With tools, the paragraph is certainly *scary*.

1. Large rats chased each other across the floor.
   a. in the dungeon
   b. searching for food

2. All was quiet.
   a. of a chain
   b. just past midnight
   c. except for the occasional rustle

3. A single set of footsteps echoed.
   a. further into the dungeon
   b. throughout the halls
   c. as someone climbed down the spiral steps
   d. through the heavy silence

4. A young woman emerged down the steps.

   a. from head to toe

   b. in a long emerald cloak

   c. dressed

5. She made her way past the row of cells.

   a. of the prisoners inside

   b. cautiously

   c. sparking the interest

6. Her pace became slower and slower.

   a. her heart beating faster and faster

   b. with every step she took

PARAGRAPH FOUR (from *Claudette Colvin: Twice Toward Justice* by Phillip Hoose)

What is the paragraph about? A major decision of the Supreme Court outlawed racial segregation in schools because of the courage of a young girl. Here's the stripped-down paragraph. Without tools, it's largely uninformative.

Without Pizzazz: The United States Supreme Court outlawed racial segregation. It was a solid punch to segregation. The ruling allowed black students to anticipate a different future. One such student was fifteen-year-old Claudette Colvin. This slim, bespectacled high school junior boarded the Highland Gardens segregated bus. She smoothed her blue dress.

With Pizzazz: Now insert the additions, and notice their power to add pizzazz to the paragraph. With tools, the paragraph is highly *informative*.

1. The United States Supreme Court outlawed racial segregation.

   a. in public schools

   b. in the case of *Brown vs. Board of Education of Topeka*

   c. on Monday, May 17, 1954

2. It was a solid punch to segregation.

   a. throughout the South

   b. one that produced shock waves

3. The ruling allowed black students to anticipate a different future

   a. to make it happen

   b. emboldening a few of them

   c. to try

4. One such student was fifteen-year-old Claudette Colvin

   a. almost nonstop

   b. whose school had been studying black history

   c. for a solid month

5. This slim, bespectacled high school junior boarded the Highland Gardens segregated bus.

   a. behind the white section of the bus

   b. and slid into a window seat on the left side

   c. around 3:30 on March 2, 1955

   d. with a few of her friends

   e. piling her textbooks on her lap

6. She smoothed her blue dress.

   a. in U.S. history

   b. and settled back

c. but would spark the most important social movement

d. for a five-block ride

e. that not only would change the course of her life

PARAGRAPH FIVE (from *Bunnicula: A Rabbit-Tale of Mystery* by Deborah and James Howe)

What is the paragraph about? A scary story told by a pet dog, this excerpt describes the night Mr. Monroe brought home a very scary rabbit. Here's the stripped-down paragraph. Without tools, the paragraph is so boring.

Without Pizzazz: It was cold. I was lying on the rug. My friend Chester the cat was curled up. I saw that once again Chester had covered the whole seat. There is nothing. The front door flew open. He unwrapped the blanket.

With Pizzazz: Now insert the additions, and notice their power to add pizzazz to the paragraph. With tools, the paragraph is very *interesting*.

---

1. It was cold.

   a. the wind howling

   b. so it felt pretty good to be indoors

   c. and the rain was pelting the windows

2. I was lying on the rug.

   a. at the front door

   b. just staring absently

   c. with my head in my paws

3. My friend Chester the cat was curled up.

    a. on the brown velvet armchair

    b. as his own

    c. which years ago he had staked out

4. I saw that once again Chester had covered the whole seat.

    a. picturing the scene tomorrow

    b. with his cat hair

    c. and I chuckled to myself

5. There is nothing.

    a. a vacuum cleaner

    b. that frightens Chester more than

    c. next to grasshoppers

6. The front door flew open.

    a. showing a flash of lightning

    b. and in its glare I noticed that Mr. Monroe was carrying a little package

    c. after a moment

    d. a blanketed bundle with tiny glistening eyes

7. He unwrapped the blanket.

    a. filled with dirt

    b. was a tiny black and white rabbit

    c. and there in the center

    d. sitting in a shoebox

EXERCISE 2: ADDING PIZZAZZ

In the paragraphs that follow, the author's additions have been removed. Pretend you are the author's partner. As coauthor, your job is to add sentence parts to add pizzazz to the paragraph. The number of words in the basic paragraph and the original paragraph is provided. Through your addition of sentence parts, try to reach roughly that number.

EXAMPLE: VIEW OF THE CITY OF SAN FRANCISCO

Basic Paragraph

Without Pizzazz: (1) He scanned his surroundings. (2) Golden hills rolled inland. (3) The flatlands of Berkeley and Oakland marched west. (4) San Francisco Bay glittered under a silvery haze. (5) A wall of fog had swallowed most of San Francisco.

Original Paragraph

With Pizzazz: (1) He scanned his surroundings. (2) **To his left**, golden hills rolled inland, **dotted with lakes, woods, and a few herds of cows.** (3) **To his right**, the flatlands of Berkeley and Oakland marched west, **a vast checkerboard of neighborhoods, with several million people who probably did not want their morning interrupted by two monsters and a filthy demigod.** (4) **Farther west**, San Francisco Bay glittered under a silvery haze. (5) **Past that**, a wall of fog had swallowed most of San Francisco, **leaving just the tops of skyscrapers and towers of the Golden Gate Bridge.**

Rick Riordan, *The Son of Neptune*

Note: The basic paragraph has forty-four words. The original paragraph has ninety-one words, <u>twice as many as the basic paragraph</u>.

PARAGRAPH ONE: CUTTING HER HAIR IN SECRET

(1) I asked Mother if I could cut off my hair. (2) She said no. (3) I found this manifestly unfair. (4) Every week I would cut off an inch of hair so that Mother wouldn't notice.

Jacqueline Kelly, *The Evolution of Calpurnia Tate*

Note: The basic paragraph has thirty-three words. The original paragraph has seventy-five words, <u>twice as many as the basic paragraph</u>.

PARAGRAPH TWO: VOLDEMORT'S GIANT SNAKE

(1) Something heavy could be heard sliding across the floor beneath the table. (2) The huge snake emerged to climb slowly up Voldemort's chair. (3) It rose. (4) Voldemort stroked the creature absently with long thin fingers.

J. K. Rowling, *Harry Potter and the Deathly Hallows*

Note: The basic paragraph has thirty-three words. The original paragraph has sixty-four words, <u>almost twice as many as the basic paragraph</u>.

PARAGRAPH THREE: A VERY MUDDY VILLAGE

(1) The village was a shade of faded brown. (2) This was because the land around the village was hard and poor. (3) The fields had to be flooded with water. (4) The villagers had to tramp in the mud. (5) Working in the mud so much made it spread everywhere.

Grace Lin, *Where the Mountain Meets the Moon*

Note: The basic paragraph has forty-six words. The original paragraph has eighty-six words, <u>almost twice as many as the basic paragraph</u>.

PARAGRAPH FOUR: WILD ANIMALS READY TO ATTACK

(1) They were not long in the mountains before Larch accepted that it was an impossible hiding place. (2) It wasn't the cold that was the problem. (3) It wasn't the terrain either. (4) It was the predators. (5) Not a week went by that Larch didn't have to defend against some attack. (6) Some of the creatures were territorial, all of them were vicious, and all of them were starving. (7) Their horse was lost one day to a pair of mountain lions.

Kristin Cashore, *Fire*

Note: The basic paragraph has seventy-nine words. The original paragraph has one hundred thirty-six words, <u>almost twice as many as the basic paragraph</u>.

PARAGRAPH FIVE: GREED FOR GOLD

(1) The Spanish conqueror Pizarro in the 16th century held the Inca king hostage for a ransom of gold. (2) No one will ever again see that life-size golden world. (3) Pizarro's men melted all those beautiful golden sculptures into boring Spanish coins and shipped boatloads of them back to the king and queen of Spain.

Jack Gantos, *Dead End in Norvelt*

Note: The basic paragraph has fifty-three words. The original paragraph has 129 words, <u>more than twice as many as the basic paragraph</u>.

EXERCISE 3: THE MISSING PARAGRAPH

In this exercise, you will continue your partnership with an author to write paragraphs with pizzazz. Each excerpt below is a series of three paragraphs. One paragraph, though, is missing. Your job, as coauthor, is to create the missing paragraph.

Study your author's two paragraphs for what they say (content) and how they say it (style). Then create the missing paragraph, making sure what you say and how you say it matches the way your partner—the original author—wrote the other two paragraphs.

Compose your paragraph of <u>at least five sentences</u>, each one with pizzazz!

PARAGRAPH SERIES ONE (from *The Great Unexpected* by Sharon Creech)

Paragraph One: If you have never had a body fall out of a tree and knock you over, let me tell you what a surprising thing it is. I have had nuts fall out of a tree and conk my head. Leaves have fallen on me, and twigs, and a branch during a storm, but never a dead body. That is not your usual thing dropping out of a tree.

Paragraph Two: <u>Write a paragraph about the boy who fell to insert here</u>.

Paragraph Three: I didn't recognize him. My first thought was, *Is this my fault? I bet this is my fault.* Nula once said I had a knack for being around when trouble happened. She had not been around other kids much, though, and maybe did not know that *most* kids had a knack for being around when trouble happened.

PARAGRAPH SERIES TWO (from *Coraline* by Neil Gaiman)

Paragraph One: That night, Coraline lay awake in her bed. The rain had stopped, and she was almost asleep when something made a noise. She sat up in bed. Coraline got out of bed and looked down the hall, but saw nothing strange. She walked down the hall. Something moved.

Paragraph Two: It was little more than a shadow, and it scuttled down the darkened hall fast, like a little patch of night. She hoped it wasn't a spider. Spiders made Coraline intensely uncomfortable. The black shape went into the next room, and Coraline followed it a little nervously into the darkened room.

Paragraph Three: <u>Write a paragraph about the black shape to insert here</u>.

PARAGRAPH SERIES THREE (from *Pollyanna* by Eleanor H. Porter)

Paragraph One: It did not take long for the entire town to learn that the doctor had said Pollyanna would never walk again. Certainly never before had the town been so stirred. Everybody knew by sight now the little freckled face that had always a smile of greeting. To think that now never again would that smiling face be seen on their streets, never again would that cheery little voice proclaim the gladness of some everyday experience! It seemed unbelievable, impossible, cruel.

Paragraph Two: Write a paragraph about the people saddened by the news to insert here.

Paragraph Three: Some came into Pollyanna's house and sat down for a stiff five or ten minutes. Some stood awkwardly on the porch steps, fumbling with hats or hand-bags. Some brought a book, a bunch of flowers, or a dainty to tempt the palate. Some cried frankly. Some turned their backs and blew their noses furiously. All inquired very anxiously for the little injured girl, and all sent to Pollyanna some message.

PARAGRAPH SERIES FOUR (from *The Silver Chair* by C. S. Lewis)

Paragraph One: There was a high stone wall, and in that wall a door by which you could get out. This door was nearly always locked, but if it should happen to be unlocked it would be a splendid way of getting outside the school grounds without being seen. He put his hand on the handle, and the handle turned, and the door opened.

Paragraph Two: What the children saw was quite different from what they had expected. They had expected to see the gray, heathery slope of the moor going up and up to join the dull autumn sky, but instead, what they saw was amazing.

Paragraph Three: Write a paragraph about the amazing scene to insert here.

PARAGRAPH SERIES FIVE (from *The Black Pearl* by Scott O'Dell)

Paragraph One: Everyone who lives in our town of La Paz has heard of the Manta Diablo. There are many people in the town who say they have seen the Manta Diablo. Old men around the fires at night tell their grandsons of the meetings they have had with him. Mothers seek to frighten bad children by threatening to call from the deeps of the sea this fearsome giant.

Paragraph Two: I am now sixteen, but when I was younger and did things I should not have done, my own mother told me that Manta Diablo was larger than the largest ship in the harbor. His eyes were the color of ambergris and shaped like a sickle moon, and there were seven of them. He had seven rows of teeth in his mouth, each tooth as long as my father's Toledo knife. With these teeth he would snap my bones like sticks.

Paragraph Three: Write a paragraph about how other mothers described a different monster to insert here.

BEYOND THE PARAGRAPH

Choose and copy one of the starter paragraphs that follow for the first paragraph of a story you create. After that paragraph, add at least five paragraphs continuing the story that began in the first paragraph.

- **PLAN** for writing the rest of your story by listing topics for several more paragraphs.

- **DRAFT** your story by writing at least one paragraph for each of those topics.

- **REWRITE** your story several times because good writers know that the best writing is the result of rewriting.

- **SHARE** your story with one or more classmates for peer review. Ask them to tell or write what they like about the story and what changes would make the story better.

- **REVISE** your story, using their comments, until it is as good as you can make it.

- **PUBLISH** your story by reading it aloud, or making paper copies for your classmates, or putting it online, or emailing it to classmates, friends, or family members.

Always Remember and Practice This Advice: Good writing results from rewriting. Rewrite your paragraph again and again, and then some more, until it's terrific!

STARTER PARAGRAPHS

1. I was staring into the hissing face of a cobra. A surprisingly pink tongue slithered in and out of a cruel mouth while an Indian man whose eyes were the blue of blindness inclined his head toward my mother and explained in Hindi that cobras make very good eating.

   (First person)

   Libba Bray, *A Great and Terrible Beauty*

2. Way out at the end of a tiny little town was an overgrown garden, and in the garden was an old house, and in the house lived a little girl. She was nine years old, and she lived there all alone. She had no mother and no father, and that was of course very nice because there was no one there to tell her to go to bed just when she was having the most fun, and no one who could make her take cod liver oil when she much preferred caramel candy.

   (Third person)

   Astrid Lindgren, *Pippi Longstocking*

3. The downpour turned into a steady cold rain. After the rain, a steady fog settled into the creek valley. It felt late for two o'clock in the afternoon. From their shelter under the bluff, they watched the creek rise up and up, ever closer to their hideout. The flood both frightened and exhilarated them. Crooked Creek looked like the Mississippi River. The brown churning water spread like long fingers

   (Third person)
   (descriptive paragraph)

into the forest on both sides of the creek. Leaves, limbs, and trees surged downstream.

Erik Masterson, The Curse of the Zombie Zoo

4. Something had happened to the night. The star-strewn indigo sky was suddenly pitch-black and lightless. The stars, the moon, the misty streetlamps at either end of the alley had vanished. The distant grumble of cars and the whisper of trees had gone. The balmy evening was suddenly piercingly, bitingly cold. They were surrounded by total, impenetrable, silent darkness, as though some giant had dropped a thick, icy mantle over the entire alley, blinding them.

(third person)

(Lots of description)

J. K. Rowling, Harry Potter and the Order of the Phoenix

5. The horses glinted in the moonlight, their riders standing tall in the saddle, swords raised. Behind them two ranks of diesel-powered walking machines stood ready to fire, canon aimed over the heads of the cavalry. A zeppelin scouted the center of the battlefield, its metal skin sparkling.

(Third person)

(Action filled)

Scott Westerfeld, Leviathan

6. The bedroom was a warm, comfortable room of doors and wood and pictures. From it, a person could reach the front or the side porch, the kitchen, and the two other bedrooms. Its walls were made of smooth oak, and on them hung gigantic photographs of Grandpa and Big Ma, Papa and Uncle Hammer when they were boys, Papa's two eldest brothers, who were now dead, and pictures of Mama's family. The furniture, a mixture of walnut and oak, included a walnut bed whose ornate headboard rose halfway up the wall toward the high ceiling, a grand chest of drawers with a floor-length mirror, a rolltop desk which had once been Grandpa's but now belonged to Mama, and four oak chairs, two of them rockers, which Grandpa had made for Big Ma as a wedding present.

(descriptive paragraph)

Mildred D. Taylor, Roll of Thunder, Hear My Cry

7. Frederic shrieked as he saw the tiger's open mouth coming at him.
When the tiger snatched him up into its maw, Frederic was too
terrified to realize that the animal had no teeth. The big cat calmly
carried the limp, weeping boy back to its cage and set him down
gently on the floor, which is what it had been carefully trained to do.
The tiger was El Strip, no ordinary tiger, the talented and coopera-
tive star of the Flimsham Brothers Circus. The Flimshams were
famous for their visually horrifying, but impressively safe, act in
which El Stripo's trainer would stuff the tiger's mouth with up to five
infants from the audience and then instruct the animal to spit them
back to their mothers. Almost always, the babies landed in the correct
laps, unharmed.

Christopher Healey, *The Hero's Guide to Saving Your Kingdom*

(narrative paragraph)

I never leave a sentence or a paragraph
until I'm satisfied with it.

—Clifford Geertz, author

PARTYING WITH SENTENCES AND PARAGRAPHS

Look closely at the word *pizzazz*. What five-letter word does it contain? Right! P-I-Z-Z-A! Like pizza, sentences and paragraphs taste good, too.

Enjoy your paragraph pizzazz party in everything you write. Thanks for coming to the party.

I pop a beautiful sentence or paragraph into my mouth and suck it like a fruit drop.

—Bohumil Hrabal, author

THANKING YOUR WRITING FITNESS TRAINERS

Over three hundred titles are the basis for the exercises in *Paragraphs for Elementary School: A Sentence-Composing Approach*, from authors who provided a training program for you to build stronger sentence and paragraph muscles. They helped you, so mentally thank them.

To remain fit, you must keep exercising. Stay in shape by reading some of their complete stories from the list, learning even more about how they build strong sentences and paragraphs. Your writing muscles (and reading muscles) will be even stronger.

Alan Armstrong, *Whittington*

Alexander Key, *The Forgotten Door*

Amar'e Stoudemire, *STAT: Home Court*

Anna Sewell, *Black Beauty*

Anne Ursu, *Breadcrumbs*

Antoine de Saint-Exupéry, *The Little Prince*

Astrid Lindgren, *Pippi Longstocking*

Avi, *Crispin: The Cross of Lead*

Barbara Brooks Wallace, *Peppermints in the Parlor*

Barbara Hattemer, "Media and Our Youth"

Becca Fitzpatrick, *Hush, Hush*

Betsy Byars, *The Night Swimmers*

Betsy Byars, *The Summer of the Swans*

Beverly Cleary, *Beezus and Ramona*

Beverly Cleary, *The Mouse and the Motorcycle*

Beverly Cleary, *Ramona and Her Father*

Beverly Cleary, *Ribsy*

Bill Brittain, *The Wish Giver*

Bill and Vera Cleaver, *Where the Lilies Bloom*

Bohumil Hrabal (quoted)

Brian Selznick, *Wonderstruck*

C. S. Lewis, *The Lion, the Witch, and the Wardrobe*

C. S. Lewis, *Prince Caspian*

C. S. Lewis, *The Silver Chair*

Carl Hiaasen, *Flush*

Carolyn Keene, *The Bungalow Mystery*

Carolyn Keene, *The Secret of Shadow Ranch*

Catherynne M. Valente, *The Girl Who Circumnavigated Fairyland in a Ship of Her Own Making*

Chris Colfer, *The Land of Stories: The Wishing Well*

Christopher Healey, *The Hero's Guide to Saving Your Kingdom*

Christopher Paolini, *Eragon*

Christopher Paolini, *Inheritance*

Chris Van Allsburg, *The Sweetest Fig*

Clair Bee, *Strike Three!*

Clare Vanderpool, *Moon Over Manifest*

Clare Vanderpool, *Navigating Early*

Clifford Geertz (quoted)

Cressida Cowell, *How to Train Your Dragon*

Cynthia Voigt, *Homecoming*

Deborah and James Howe, *Bunnicula: A Rabbit-Tale of Mystery*

Dick King-Smith, *Pigs Might Fly*

Earline Moses (quoted)

E. B. White, *Charlotte's Web*

E. B. White, *Stuart Little*

E. B. White, *The Trumpet of the Swan*

Edmund Ware, "An Underground Episode"

Edward Bloor, *Tangerine*

Eleanor Coerr, *Sadako and the Thousand Paper Cranes*

Eleanor Estes, *Ginger Pye*

Eleanor H. Porter, *Pollyanna*

E. L. Konigsburg, *From the Mixed-Up Files of Mrs. Basil E. Frankweiler*

Elizabeth George Speare, *The Bronze Bow*

Elizabeth George Speare, *The Witch of Blackbird Pond*

Enid Bagnold, *National Velvet*

Eoin Colfer, *Artemis Fowl*

Eric P. Kelly, *The Trumpeter of Krakow*

Erik Masterson, *The Curse of the Zombie Zoo*

Ernesto Galarza, *Barrio Boy*

Esther Averill, *Jenny and the Cat Club*

Esther Hoskins Forbes, *Johnny Tremain*

Ezra Jack Keats, *The Snowy Day*

Fanny Billingsley, *Chime*

Frances Hodgson Burnett, *A Little Princess*

Franklin W. Dixon, *The Secret of the Old Mill*

Franklin W. Dixon, *The Tower Treasure*

Gail Carson Levine, *Ella Enchanted*

Gary Paulsen, *Hatchet*

Gary Paulsen, *The Monument*

Gary Paulsen, *The Time Hackers*

Gary Paulsen, *Wood-Song*

Gene Olson, *The Roaring Road*

Gene Zion, "Harry the Dirty Dog"

Gertrude Chandler Warner, *The Boxcar Children*

Grace Lin, *Where the Mountain Meets the Moon*

Hans Augusto Rey, *Curious George*

Harry Allard, *Miss Nelson Is Missing!*

Heywood Broun, "The Fifty-First Dragon"

J. K. Rowling, *Harry Potter and the Chamber of Secrets*

J. K. Rowling, *Harry Potter and the Deathly Hallows*

J. K. Rowling, *Harry Potter and the Goblet of Fire*

J. K. Rowling, *Harry Potter and the Half-Blood Prince*

J. K. Rowling, *Harry Potter and the Order of the Phoenix*

J. K. Rowling, *Harry Potter and the Prisoner of Azkaban*

J. K. Rowling, *Harry Potter and the Sorcerer's Stone*

J. M. Barrie, *Peter Pan*

J. R. R. Tolkien, *The Fellowship of the Ring*

J. R. R. Tolkien, *The Hobbit*

Jack Gantos, *Dead End in Norvelt*

Jack London, "To Build a Fire"

Jacqueline Davies, *The Lemonade War*

Jacqueline Kelly, *The Evolution of Calpurnia Tate*

James Hurst, "The Scarlet Ibis"

Janell Cannon, *Stellaluna*

Jean Craighead George, *The Fire Bug Connection*

Jean Craighead George, *Julie of the Wolves*

Jean Craighead George, *The Missing 'Gator of Gumbo Limbo*

Jean Craighead George, *My Side of the Mountain*

Jean Craighead George, *The Talking Earth*

Jean Merrill, *The Pushcart War*

Jennifer A. Nielsen, *The False Prince*

Jerry Spinelli, *Knots in My Yo-Yo String*

Jerry Spinelli, *Maniac Magee*

Jim Murphy, *The Great Fire*

John Christopher, *The Guardians*

John R. Tunis, *All American*

John R. Tunis, *World Series*

Joseph Delaney, *The Last Apprentice*

Joseph Krumgold, *. . . And Now Miguel*

K. A. Applegate, *Animorphs: The Underground*

Kate DiCamillo, *Because of Winn-Dixie*

Kate DiCamillo, *The Miraculous Journey of Edward Tulane*

Kate DiCamillo, *The Tale of Despereaux*

Kate DiCamillo, *The Tiger Rising*

Katherine Paterson, *Bridge to Terabithia*

Kenneth Grahame, *The Wind in the Willows*

Kip Taylor, *Finn Flanagan and the Fledglings*

Kristin Cashore, *Fire*

Langston Hughes, "Thank You, M'am"

Larry Scheckel, *Ask Your Science Teacher*

Laura Ingalls Wilder, *Little House on the Prairie*

Laurel Snyder, *Bigger Than a Bread Box*

Laurence Yep, *Dragon of the Lost Sea*

Lemony Snicket, *The Bad Beginning*

Lemony Snicket, *The End*

Lemony Snicket, *Who Could That Be at This Hour?*

Leo Lionni, *Swimmy*

Leon Hugo, "My Father and the Hippopotamus"

Leslie Morris, "Three Shots for Charlie Beston"

Lewis Carroll, *Alice's Adventures in Wonderland*

L. Frank Baum, *The Wonderful Wizard of Oz*

Libba Bray, *A Great and Terrible Beauty*

Linda Sue Park, *A Single Shard*

Linda Urban, *Hound Dog True*

Lloyd Alexander, *The Book of Three*

Lois Duncan, *A Gift of Magic*

Lois Lenski, *Strawberry Girl*

Lois Lowry, *The Giver*

Lois Lowry, *Number the Stars*

Louis Sachar, *Holes*

Louis Sachar, *There's a Boy in the Girl's Bathroom*

Louise Fitzhugh, *Harriet the Spy*

Louise Fitzhugh, *The Long Secret*

Lynne Rae Perkins, *Criss Cross*

Lynne Reid Banks, *The Indian in the Cupboard*

Lynne Reid Banks, *One More River*

Madeleine L'Engle, *A Swiftly Tilting Planet*

Madeleine L'Engle, *A Wind in the Door*

Madeleine L'Engle, *A Wrinkle in Time*

Margaret Peterson Haddix, *Among the Hidden*

Margarita Engle, *The Firefly Letters*

Margery Williams, *The Velveteen Rabbit*

Marguerite Henry, *Misty of Chincoteague*

Marjorie Kinnan Rawlings, *The Yearling*

Maurice Sendak, *Where the Wild Things Are*

Megan Whalen Turner, *The King of Atollia*

Michael Crichton, *Jurassic Park*

Michael Morpurgo, *War Horse*

Mildred D. Taylor, *Roll of Thunder, Hear My Cry*

Munro Leaf, *The Story of Ferdinand*

Murray Heyert, "The New Kid"

Nancy Farmer, *The House of the Scorpion*

Neil Gaiman, *Coraline*

Neil Gaiman, *The Graveyard Book*

Norah Burke, "Polar Night"

Norton Juster, *The Phantom Tollbooth*

Olive Ann Burns, *Cold Sassy Tree*

Orson Scott Card, *Ender's Game*

Pam Conrad, "The Tub People"

Pam Muñoz Ryan, *Esperanza Rising*

Pat Conroy, *My Reading Life*

Patricia A. Halbert (editor), *I Wish I Knew That: U.S. Presidents*

Patricia C. McKissack, *A Million Fish . . . More or Less*

Patricia MacLachlan, *Sarah, Plain and Tall*

Patrick Ness, *A Monster Calls*

Peter Lerangis, *39 Clues*

Philip Pullman, *The Golden Compass*

Phillip Hoose, *Claudette Colvin: Twice Toward Justice*

Phyllis Reynolds Naylor, *Shiloh*

Post Wheeler, *Vasilissa the Beautiful*

R. J. Palacio, *Wonder*

R. L. Stine, *Ghost Beach*

Rachel Carson, *The Edge of the Sea*

Randall Jarrell, *The Bat Poet*

Ray Bradbury, "The Whole Town's Sleeping"

Rebecca Stead, *When You Reach Me*

Richard Adams, *Watership Down*

Richard Connell, "The Most Dangerous Game"
Rick Riordan, *The Lightning Thief*
Rick Riordan, *A Maze of Bones*
Rick Riordan, *The Son of Neptune*
Rita Williams-Garcia, *One Crazy Summer*
Roald Dahl, *The BFG*
Roald Dahl, *Charlie and the Chocolate Factory*
Roald Dahl, *Fantastic Mr. Fox*
Roald Dahl, *Matilda*
Roald Dahl, *The Witches*
Robert C. O'Brien, *Mrs. Frisby and the Rats of NIMH*
Robert Lipsyte, *The Contender*
Roger Duvoisin, "Petunia"
Roland Smith, *Peak*
Rosa Guy, *Edith Jackson*
Sarah Dessen, *Dreamland*
Scott O'Dell, *The Black Pearl*
Scott O'Dell, *Island of the Blue Dolphins*
Scott Westerfeld, *Goliath*
Scott Westerfeld, *Leviathan*
Sharon Creech, *The Great Unexpected*
Sharon Creech, *Walk Two Moons*
Sheila Burnford, *The Incredible Journey*
Steve Sheinkin, *Bomb*
Susan Patron, *The Higher Power of Lucky*
Suzanne Collins, *Catching Fire*
Suzanne Collins, *The Hunger Games*
Suzanne Collins, *Mockingjay*
Terry Pratchett, *Dodger*
Thomas Rockwell, *How to Eat Fried Worms*
Thornton Wilder (quoted)
Tom Wolfe, *A Man in Full*
Toni Cade Bambara, "Geraldine Moore the Poet"